IGOR STRAVINSKY

IGOR STRAVINSKY, probably the most renowned composer of the twentieth century, was born in 1882 in Oranienbaum, near St. Petersburg, Russia, and studied composition with Rimsky-Korsakov. He won world-wide recognition for his ballets commissioned by Diaghilev, including *The Firebird, Petrushka,* and *The Rite of Spring.* He left Russia and for many years lived in France and Switzerland, later moving to the United States, where he died in 1971. Among his many compositions are the opera *The Rake's Progress,* the oratorio *Oedipus Rex, Persephone, Symphony of Psalms, Threni, Symphony in C, Symphony in 3 Movements,* and works for ballet introduced by Balanchine, including *Apollo, Orpheus,* and *Agon.* In addition to *An Autobiography,* completed in 1934, he was also the author of *Poetics of Music.* Six volumes of dialogues and other material, prepared in collaboration with Robert Craft, were also published: *Conversations with Igor Stravinsky, Memories and Commentaries, Expositions and Developments, Dialogues and a Diary, Themes and Episodes,* and *Retrospectives and Conclusions.*

An Autobiography

IGOR STRAVINSKY

An Autobiography

W. W. NORTON & COMPANY
New York · London

ISBN 0-393-31856-7

W. W. Norton & Company, Inc., 500 Fifth Avenue, New York, NY 10110
http://www.wwnorton.com

W. W. Norton & Company Ltd., 10 Coptic Street, London WC1A 1PU

2 3 4 5 6 7 8 9 0

Foreword

Foreword

The aim of this volume is to set down a few recollections connected with various periods of my life. It is equally intended for those interested in my music and in myself. Rather, therefore, than a biography it will be a simple account of important events side by side with facts of minor consequence: both, however, have a certain significance for me, and I wish to relate them according to the dictates of my memory.

Naturally I shall not be able to keep within the bounds of bare statement. As I call my recollections to mind, I shall necessarily be obliged to speak of my opinions, my tastes, my preferences, and my abhorrences.

I am but too well aware of how much these feelings vary in the course of time. This is why I shall take great care not to confuse my present reactions with those experienced at other stages in my life.

There are still further reasons which induce me to write this book. In numerous interviews I have given, my thoughts, my words, and even facts have often been disfigured to the extent of becoming absolutely unrecognizable.

I therefore undertake this task today in order to present to the reader a true picture of myself, and to dissipate the accumulation of misunderstandings that has gathered about both my work and my person.

ONE: *Development of the Composer*

I

As memory reaches back along the vista of the years, the increasing distance adds to the difficulty of seeing clearly and choosing between those incidents which make a deep impression and those which, though perhaps more important in themselves, leave no trace, and in no way influence one's development.

Thus, one of my earliest memories of sound will seem somewhat odd.

It was in the country, where my parents, like most people of their class, spent the summer with their children. I can see it now. An enormous peasant seated on the stump of a tree. The sharp resinous tang of fresh-cut wood in my nostrils. The peasant simply clad in a short red shirt. His bare legs covered with reddish hair, on his feet birch sandals, on his head a mop of hair as thick and as red as his beard – not a white hair, yet an old man.

He was dumb, but he had a way of clicking his tongue very noisily, and the children were afraid of him. So was I. But curiosity used to triumph over fear. The children would gather round him. Then, to amuse them, he would begin to sing. This song was composed of two syllables, the only ones he could pronounce. They were devoid of any meaning, but he made them alternate with incredible dexterity in a very rapid tempo. He used to accompany this clucking in the following way: pressing the palm of his right hand under his left armpit, he would work his left arm with a rapid movement, making it press on the right hand. From beneath the red shirt he extracted a succession of sounds which were somewhat dubious but very rhythmic, and which might be euphemistically described as resounding kisses. This amused me beyond words, and at home I set myself with zeal to imitate this music – so often and so successfully that I was forbidden to indulge in such an indecent accompaniment. The two dull syllables which alone remained thus lost all their attraction for me.

Another memory which often comes back is the singing of the women of the neighboring village. There were a great many of them, and regularly every evening they sang in unison on their way home after the day's work. To this day I clearly remember the tune, and the way they sang it, and how, when I used to sing it at home, imitating their manner, I was complimented on the trueness of my ear. This praise made me very happy.

And it is an odd thing that this occurrence, trifling though it seems, has a special significance for me, because it marks the dawn of my consciousness of myself in the role of musician.

I will confine myself to those two impressions of summer, which was always associated with a picture of the country, and of all the things to be seen and heard there.

Winter was quite another story – town. My memories of that do not go so far back as those of summer, and I date them from the time when I was about three years old. Winter, with its curtailing of liberty and amusements, with its rigorous discipline and interminable length, was not likely to make enduring impressions.

4

My parents were not specially concerned with my musical development until I was nine. It is true that there was music in the house, my father being the leading bass singer of the Imperial Opera in St. Petersburg, but I heard all this music only at a distance – from the nursery to which my brothers and I were relegated.

When I was nine my parents gave me a piano mistress. I very quickly learned to read music, and, as the result of reading, soon had a longing to improvise, a pursuit to which I devoted myself, and which for a long time was my favorite occupation. There cannot have been anything very interesting in these improvisations, because I was frequently reproached for wasting my time in that way instead of practicing properly, but I was definitely of a different opinion, and the reproaches vexed me considerably. Although today I understand and admit the need of this discipline for a child of nine or ten, I must say that my constant work at improvisation was not absolutely fruitless; for, on the one hand, it contributed to my better knowledge of the piano, and, on the other, it sowed the seed of musical ideas. Apropos of this, I should like to quote a remark of Rimsky-Korsakov's that he made later on when I became his pupil. I asked him whether I was right in always composing at the piano. "Some compose at the piano," he replied, "and some without a piano. As for you, you will compose at the piano." As a matter of fact, I do compose at the piano and I do not regret it. I go further; I think it is a thousand times better to compose in direct contact with the physical medium of sound than to work in the abstract medium produced by one's imagination.

Apart from my improvisation and piano-practice, I found immense pleasure in reading the opera scores of which my father's library consisted – all the more so because I was able to read with great facility. My mother also had that gift, and I must have inherited it from her. Imagine my joy, therefore, when for the first time I was taken to the theatre where they were giving an opera with which as a pianist I was already familiar. It was *A Life for the Tsar*, and it was then I heard an orchestra for the first time. And what an orchestra – Glinka's! The impression was indelible, but it must not be supposed that this was due solely to the fact that it was the first orchestra I ever heard. To this day, not only Glinka's music in itself, but his orchestration as well, remains a perfect monument of musical art – so intelligent is his balance of tone, so distinguished and delicate his instrumentation; and by the latter I mean his choice of instruments and his way of combining them. I was indeed fortunate in happening on a *chef d'oeuvre* for my first contact with great music. That is why my attitude towards Glinka has always been one of unbounded gratitude.

I remember having heard another lyrical work that same winter, but it was by a composer of the second rank – Alexander Serov – and on that occasion I was impressed only by the dramatic action. My father had the leading part, a role in which he was particularly admired by the Petersburg public. He was a very well-known artist in his day. He had a beautiful voice and an amazing technique, acquired in studying by the Italian method at the St. Petersburg Conservatoire, in addition to great dramatic talent – a rare attribute among opera singers at that time.

About the same time I heard Glinka's second opera, *Ruslan and Ludmilla*, at a gala performance given to celebrate its fiftieth anniversary. My father took the part of Farlaf, which was one of the best in his repertoire. It was a memorable evening for me. Besides the excitement I felt at

6

hearing this music that I already loved to distraction, it was my good fortune to catch a glimpse in the foyer of Peter Tchaikovsky, the idol of the Russian public, whom I had never seen before and was never to see again. He had just conducted the first audition of his new symphony – the *Pathetic* – in St. Petersburg. A fortnight later my mother took me to a concert where the same symphony was played in memory of its composer, who had been suddenly carried off by cholera. Deeply though I was impressed by the unexpected death of the great musician, I was far from realizing at the moment that this glimpse of the living Tchaikovsky – fleeting though it was – would become one of my most treasured memories. I shall have occasion later to tell my readers more of Tchaikovsky, of his music, and of my struggles on its behalf with some of my confreres, who obstinately persist in a heresy which will not permit them to recognize as "authentic" Russian music anything outside the work of the Five (*name given to a group composed of Balakirev, Moussorgsky, Borodin, Rimsky-Korsakov, and Cui*).

At this point I am simply recording a personal memory of the celebrated composer, for whom my admiration has continued to grow with the development of my musical consciousness.

I think that the beginning of my conscious life as artist and musician dates from this time.

II

I picture the first years of my adolescence as a series of irksome duties and the perpetual frustration of all my desires and aspirations. The constraint of the school to which I had just gone filled me with aversion. I hated the classes and tasks, and I was but a very poor pupil, my lack of industry giving rise to reproaches which only increased my dislike for the school and its lessons. Nor did I find any compensation for all this unpleasantness in those school friendships which might have made things easier. During all my school life, I never came across anyone who had any real attraction for me, something essential being always absent. Was it my fault, or was it simply bad luck? I cannot say; but the result was that I felt very lonely. Although I was brought up with my younger brother, of whom I was very fond, I was never able to open my heart to him, because, in the first place, my aspirations were too vague to be formulated, and secondly, in my innermost being I feared, notwithstanding our mutual affection, that there would be misunderstandings which would have deeply wounded my pride.

The only place where my budding ambition had any encouragement was in the house of my uncle Ielatchitch, my mother's brother-in-law. Both he and his children were fervent music lovers, with a general tendency to champion very advanced work, or what was then considered to be such. My uncle belonged to the class of society then predominating in St. Petersburg, which was composed of well-to-do land-owners, officials of the higher ranks, magistrates, barristers, and the like. They all prided themselves on their liberalism, extolled progress, and considered it the thing to profess so-called "advanced" opinions in politics, art, and all branches of social life. The reader can easily see from this what their mentality was like: a compulsory atheism, a somewhat bold affirmation of "the Rights of Man," an attitude of opposition to "tyrannical" government, the cult of materialistic science, and, at the same time, admiration for Tolstoy and his amateur Christianizing. Special artistic tastes went with this mentality, and it is easy to see what they looked for and appreciated in music. Obviously naturalism was the order of the day, pushed to the point of realistic expression and accompanied, as was to be expected, by popular and nationalistic tendencies and admiration for folklore. And it was on such grounds that these sincere music lovers believed that they must justify their enthusiasm – quick and spontaneous though it was – for works of a Moussorgsky!

It would, however, be unfair to imply that this set had no appreciation of symphonic music; Brahms was admired, and a little later Bruckner was discovered, and a special transcription of Wagner's tetralogy was played as a pianoforte duet. Was it Glazounov, adopted son of the Five, with his heavy German academic symphonies, or the lyrical symphonies of Tchaikovsky, or the epic symphonies of Borodin, or the symphonic poems of Rimsky-Korsakov, that imbued this group with its taste for symphonism? Who can say? But, however that may be, all these ardently devoted themselves to that type of music.

It was thanks to this environment that I got to know the great German composers. As for the French moderns; they had not yet penetrated into this circle, and it was only later that I had a chance to hear them.

In so far as school life permitted, I used to go to symphony concerts and to recitals by famous Russian or foreign pianists, and in this way I heard Josef Hofmann, whose serious, precise, and finished playing filled me with such enthusiasm that I redoubled my zeal in studying the piano. Among other celebrities who appeared in St. Petersburg at the time, I remember Sophie Menter, Eugen d'Albert, Reisenauer, and such of our own famous virtuosi as the pianist Annette Essipova, the wife of Leschetitzky, and the violinist, Leopold Auer.

There were also great symphonic concerts given by two important societies – the Imperial Musical Society and the Russian Symphony Concerts – founded by Mitrophan Belaieff, that great patron and publisher of music.

The concerts of the Imperial Society were often conducted by Napravnik, whom I already knew through the Imperial Opera, of which he was for many years the distinguished conductor. It seems to me that in spite of his austere conservatism he was the type of conductor which even today I prefer to all others. Certainty and unbending rigor in the exercise of his art; complete contempt for all affectation and showy effects alike in the presentation of the work and in gesticulation; not the slightest concession to the public; and added to that, iron discipline, mastery of the first order, an infallible ear and memory, and, as a result, perfect clarity and objectivity in the rendering. . . . What better can one imagine? Hans Richter, a much better-known and more celebrated conductor, whom I heard a little later when he came to St. Petersburg to conduct the Wagner operas, had the same qualities. He also belonged to that rare type of conductor whose sole ambition is to penetrate the spirit and the aim of the composer, and to submerge himself in the score.

I used to go also to the Belaieff Symphony Concerts. Belaieff had formed a group of musicians whom he helped in every way: giving them material assistance, publishing their works and having them performed at his concerts. The leading figures in this group were Rimsky-Korsakov and Glazounov, who were joined by Liadov and, later on, Tcherepnin, the brothers Blumenfeld, Sokolov, and other pupils of Rimsky-Korsakov. This group, though the offspring of the Five, rapidly changed, and, perhaps without realizing it, developed a new school, little by little taking possession of the Conservatoire in place of the old academicians who had directed it since its foundation by Anton Rubinstein.

When I got into touch with some of the members of this group, its transformation into a new school had already been accomplished, so that I found myself confronted by an academy whose aesthetics and dogmas were well established, and had to be accepted or rejected as a whole.

I was then of an age – the age of early apprenticeship – when the critical faculty is generally lacking, and one blindly accepts truths propounded by those whose prestige is unanimously recognized, especially when this prestige is concerned with the mastery of technique and the art of *savoir faire*. Thus I accepted their dogmas quite spontaneously, and all the more readily because at that time I was a fervent admirer of Rimsky-Korsakov and Glazounov. I was specially drawn to the former by his melodic and harmonic inspiration, which then seemed to me full of freshness; to the latter by his feeling for symphonic form; and to both by their scholarly workmanship. I need hardly stress how much I longed to attain this ideal of perfection in which I really saw the highest degree of art; and with all the feeble means at my disposal I assiduously strove to imitate them in my attempts at composition.

It was during these years that I made the acquaintance

of Ivan Pokrovsky, a young man, older than myself, highly cultured, with advanced tastes, a lover of art in general and of music in particular. My association with him was very pleasant, because it relieved the monotony of school life and at the same time extended the field of my artistic ideas. He introduced me to authors of whom, till then, I had known nothing – above all to French composers such as Gounod, Bizet, Delibes, and Chabrier. Even then I noticed a certain affinity between the music of these composers and that of Tchaikovsky, an affinity which I saw much more clearly when, later, I was able to examine and compare their works with a more practiced eye. It is true that I was familiar with those pages of *Faust* and *Carmen* which one heard everywhere, but it was chiefly the fact that I was always hearing them that had prevented me from consciously forming an opinion of these musicians. It was only on looking into their works with Pokrovsky that I discovered in them a musical language which was unfamiliar to me, and which differed noticeably from that of the Belaieff group and its kind. I found in them a different type of musical writing, different harmonic methods, a different melodic conception, a freer and fresher feeling for form. This gave rise to doubts, as yet barely perceptible, with regard to what had up till then seemed unassailable dogma. That is why I am eternally grateful to Pokrovsky; for from my discussions with him dates my gradual emancipation from the influence that, all unknown to myself, the academicism of the time was exercising over me. I must say, however, that for many years to come, in spite of everything, the domination of this group was still noticeable in me.

Indeed, I often undertook to defend the principles of the group, and in a most peremptory manner, when I came

up against the antiquated opinions of those who did not realize that they themselves had long since been left behind.
Thus I had to battle with my second piano mistress, a pupil
and admirer of Anton Rubinstein. She was an excellent
pianist and a good musician, but completely obsessed by her
adoration for her illustratious master, whose views she
blindly accepted, and I had great difficulty in making her
accept the scores of Rimsky-Korsakov or of Wagner – which
at that period I was fervently studying. But here I must say
that, notwithstanding our differences of opinion, this excellent musician managed to give a new impetus to my piano
playing and to the development of my technique. At that
moment the question of my vocation had not been raised
in any definite form either by my parents or by myself. And
how could one in fact foretell the hazardous course of a composer's career? My parents, like the majority of their class,
therefore, thought above all of giving me the education
necessary to enable me to obtain a post, administrative or
otherwise, which would assure me a livelihood. That is why,
as soon as I had matriculated, they considered it advisable
that I should study law at the University of St. Petersburg.
As for my inclinations and my predilections for music, they
regarded them as mere amateurism, to be encouraged up to
a point, without in the least taking into consideration the
degree to which my aptitudes might be developed. This now
seems to me quite natural.

The next few years, in which I had to matriculate and
then to work at the University, were, as may well be imagined, by no means attractive from my point of view, because my interests all lay elsewhere. However, at my urgent
request, my parents agreed to give me a teacher of harmony.
I therefore began the study of harmony, but, contrary to all

expectation, I found no satisfaction in it, perhaps owing to the pedagogical incompetence of my teacher, perhaps to the method used, and perhaps – and this is most likely – to my inherent aversion to any dry study. Let me make myself clear. I always did, and still do, prefer to achieve my aims and to solve any problems which confront me in the course of my work solely by my own efforts, without having recourse to established processes which do, it is true, facilitate the task, but which must first be learned and then remembered. To learn and remember such things, however useful they might be, always seemed to me dull and boring; I was too lazy for that sort of work, especially as I had little faith in my memory. If that had been better, I should certainly have found more interest, and possibly even pleasure, in it. I insist on the word "pleasure," though some people might find it too light a word for the scope and significance of the feeling I am trying to indicate.

But I can experience this feeling of pleasure in the very process of work, and in looking forward to the joy that any find or discovery may bring. And I admit that I am not sorry that this should have been so, because perfect facility would, of necessity, have diminished my eagerness in striving, and the satisfaction of having "found" would not have been complete.

On the other hand, I was much drawn to the study of counterpoint, though that is generally considered a dry subject, useful only for pedagogical purposes. From about the age of eighteen I began to study it alone, with no other help than an ordinary manual. The work amused me, even thrilled me, and I was never tired of it. This first contact with the science of counterpoint opened up at once a far vaster and more fertile field in the domain of musical composition than anything that harmony could offer me. And so I set myself with heart and soul to the task of solving the many problems it contains. This amused me tremendously, but it was only later that I realized to what an extent those exercises had helped to develop my judgment and my taste in music. They stimulated my imagination and my desire to compose; they laid the foundation of all my future technique, prepared me thoroughly for the study of form, of orchestration, and of instrument which later I took up with Rimsky-Korsakov.

I have now reached the period at which I made the acquaintance of that illustrious composer. When I went to the University I found his youngest son there, and was very soon on the best of terms with him. At that time his father hardly knew of my existence.

In 1902 Rimsky-Korsakov took his whole family to spend the summer vacation at Heidelberg, where one of his sons was a student at the University. At the same time my mother and I had gone to Bad Wildungen with my father, who was already seriously ill. From there I rushed over to Heidelberg to see my fellow student and also to consult his father about my vocation. I told him of my ambition to become a composer, and asked his advice. He made me play some of my first attempts. Alas! the way in which he received them was far from what I had hoped. Seeing how upset I was, and evidently anxious not to discourage me, he asked if I could play anything else. I did so, of course, and it was then that he gave his opinion.

He told me that before anything else I must continue my studies in harmony and counterpoint with one or other of his pupils in order to acquire complete mastery in the schooling of craftsmanship, but at the same time he strongly advised me not to enter the Conservatoire. He considered that the atmosphere of that institution, in which he was himself a professor, was not suited to me, for I should be overwhelmed with work, and he suggested I might as well go on with my University course. Moreover, as I was twenty he feared that I might find myself backward in comparison with my contemporaries, and that this might discourage me. He further considered it necessary that my work should be systematically supervised, and that this could be achieved only by private lessons. He finished by adding that I could always go to him for advice, and that he was quite willing to take me in hand when I had acquired the necessary foundation.

Although in my ingenuousness I was somewhat downcast over the lack of enthusiasm that the master had shown for my first attempts at composition, I found some comfort in the fact that he had nevertheless advised me to continue my studies, and so demonstrated his opinion that I had sufficient ability to devote myself to a musical career. This comforted me all the more because everyone knew the rigor and frankness of his judgment when his verdict as to the musical vocation of a beginner was required: he fully realized the personal responsibility attaching to his great authority. The story was told of a young doctor who came to show him his compositions and ask for advice. Having learned that he was a doctor, Rimsky-Korsakov said: "Excellent. Continue to practice medicine."

After my interview with the master I had firmly resolved to devote myself seriously to my studies with my harmony teacher, but once again I found that I was thoroughly bored, and felt that I was making scarcely any progress.

At that moment several circumstances prevented me

from working regularly. First there was the death of my father in November, 1902. Then there was the desire to live an independent life in the company of my friends, who formed an ever-widening circle, largely owing to my association with the Rimsky-Korsakov family, of whom I saw as much as possible. In this highly cultured environment I formed new ties among the young people whom I met there, all of whom had intellectual interests of one sort or another. There were painters, young scientists, scholars, enlightened amateurs of the most advanced views. One of them was my friend Stepan Mitoussov, with whom later I composed the libretto for my opera, *Le Rossignol*. We took a passionate interest in everything that went on in the intellectual and artistic life of the capital. Diaghileff had just started the publication of his vanguard review, *Mir Iskoustva* (*The World of Art*), and was organizing his exhibitions of pictures. At the same time my friends Pokrovsky, Nouvel, and Nurok founded an interesting musical society which they called Soirees of Contemporary Music. It is needless to speak of the importance of these two groups in my artistic and intellectual evolution, and how much they strengthened the development of my creative faculty.

Here I must break the thread of my story in order to acquaint the reader with the antagonism which was inevitable to arise between opinion in academic circles and the new trend in art which these two societies stood for. I will not expatiate on the aggressive hostility with which the reactionary and conservative set in the Academy and the Imperial Society for the Encouragement of Art met the activities of Diaghileff, and particularly his review, *Mir Iskoustva* – and God knows what he endured in that struggle! I will touch here only on the musicians and their attitude towards the whole of this new movement. Certainly the majority of the Conservatoire pedagogues were against it, and accused it, of course, of corrupting the taste of the younger generation. But I must say, in justice to Rimsky-Korsakov and Liadov, that, notwithstanding their disapproval, they had sufficient courage and finesse not to make a sweeping condemnation of everything serious and appreciable that modern art had to offer.

The following is illustrative of the attitude of the old master towards Debussy. At a concert where one of the latter's works was on the program I asked Rimsky-Korsakov what he thought of it. He answered in these very words: "Better not listen to him; one runs the risk of getting accustomed to him and one would end by liking him." But such was not the attitude of his disciples – they were more royalist than the King. The rare exceptions discoverable among them served only to prove the rule. My recollection of Liadov is a pleasant one. His head looked very much like that of a Kalmuck woman, and he had a gentle, agreeable, and kindly nature. Bent on clear and meticulous writing, he was very strict with his pupils and with himself, composing very little and working slowly, and, so to speak, under a microscope. He read much, and, considering the atmosphere of the Conservatoire where he was a professor, he was fairly broadminded.

It was at this period that I became acquainted with the works of César Franck, Vincent d'Indy, Fauré, Paul Dukas, and Debussy, of whose names I had hardly heard. Our Academy pretended to know nothing of all these French composers of widespread fame, and never included their works in the programs of the big symphony concerts. As the Soirees of Contemporary Music had not the wherewithal for giving orchestral performances, we were at that time able to hear only the chamber music of these composers. It was not till later, at the concerts of Siloti and those of Koussevitzky, that our public had a chance to hear their symphonic productions.

The impressions I formed of the work of these composers, so different from each other, were naturally varied. My feelings were already beginning to crystallize on the subject of César Franck and his academic thought, Vincent d'Indy and his scholastic yet Wagnerian mentality, on the one hand, and Debussy on the other, with his extraordinary freedom and freshness of technique that was really quite new for his period. Next to him Chabrier appealed most to me, notwithstanding his well-known Wagnerianism (to my mind a purely superficial and outward aspect of him), and my taste for his music has increased with time.

It must not be imagined that my inclination towards the new tendencies, of which I have just spoken, meant any diminution in my adoration for my old masters, because all the appreciations expressed above were then only subconsciously germinating, while consciously I felt an imperative need to get a foothold in my profession. I could achieve that only by submitting to the discipline of these masters, and, by implication, to their aesthetics. This discipline, while of the utmost rigor, was at the same time most productive, and it was in no way responsible for the number of mediocrities of the Prix de Rome type to which our Academy gave birth every year. But, as I have said, in submitting to their discipline I was confronted by their aesthetics, from which it could not be divorced. Indeed, every doctrine of aesthetics, when put into practice, demands a particular mode of expression -- in fact, a technique of its own; for, in art, such a thing

19

as technique founded on no given basis – in short, a technique in the void – would be utterly inconceivable; and it would be still more difficult to imagine when a whole group, or school, is under consideration. I cannot, therefore, reproach my teachers for having clung to their own aesthetics; they could not have done otherwise; and, as a matter of fact, it was no hindrance to me. On the other hand, the technical knowledge that I acquired, thanks to them, gave me a foundation of incalculable value in its solidity, on which I was able later to establish and develop my own craftsmanship. No matter what the subject may be, there is only one course for the beginner; he must at first accept a discipline imposed from without, but only as the means of obtaining freedom for, and strengthening himself in, his own method of expression.

About this time I composed a full-sized sonata for the piano. In this work I was constantly confronted by many difficulties, especially in matters of form, the mastery of which is usually acquired only after prolonged study, and my perplexities suggested the idea of my consulting Rimsky-Korsakov again. I went to see him in the country at the end of the summer of 1903, and stayed with him for about a fortnight. He made me compose the first part of a sonatina under his supervision, after having instructed me in the principles of the allegro of a sonata. He explained these principles with a lucidity so remarkable as to show me at once what a great teacher he was. At the same time he taught me the compass and the registers of the different instruments used in contemporary symphonic orchestras, and the first elements of the art of orchestration. He adopted the plan of teaching form and orchestration side by side, because in his view the more highly developed musical forms found their fullest expression in the complexity of the orchestra.

I worked with him in this way: he would give me some pages of the piano score of a new opera he had just finished (*Pan Voïvoda*), which I was to orchestrate. When I had orchestrated a section, he would show me his own instrumentation of the same passage. I had to compare them, and then he would ask me to explain why he had done it differently. Whenever I was unable to do so, it was he who explained. Thus was established our association as teacher and pupil, which, with the beginning of regular lessons in the autumn, continued for about three years.

Although he was giving me lessons, he nevertheless wanted me still to continue my studies of counterpoint with my former teacher, who was one of his pupils. But I think that he only insisted for conscience' sake, and that he realized that these lessons would not take me far. Shortly afterwards I gave them up, though that did not prevent me from continuing alone the counterpoint exercises, in which I took more and more interest, and during that period I filled a thick volume with them. Alas! it was left in my country house in Russia, where, together with my whole library, it disappeared during the Revolution.

My work with Rimsky-Korsakov consisted of his giving me pieces of classical music to orchestrate. I remember that they were chiefly parts of Beethoven's sonatas, and of Schubert's quartets and marches. Once a week I took my work to him and he criticized and corrected it, giving me all the necessary explanations, and at the same time he made me analyze the form and structure of classical works. A year and a half later I began the composition of a symphony. As soon as I finished one part of a movement I used to show it to him, so that my whole work, including the instrumentation, was under his control.

I composed this symphony at the time when Alexander

Glazounov reigned supreme in the science of symphony. Each new production of his was received as a musical event of the first order, so greatly were the perfections of his form, the purity of his counterpoint, and the ease and assurance of his writing appreciated. At that time I shared this admiration whole-heartedly, fascinated by the astonishing mastery of this scholar. It was, therefore, quite natural that side by side with other influences (Tchaikovsky, Wagner, Rimsky-Korsakov) his predominated, and that in my symphony I modeled myself particularly on him.

At this point the period of my adolescence came to an end. In the spring of 1905 I finished my University course. In the autumn I became engaged, and I was married in January, 1906.

III

After my marriage I continued my lessons with Rimsky-Korsakov, the work consisting mainly of my showing him my compositions and discussing them with him. During the season of 1906–1907, I finished my symphony and dedicated it to him. I composed also a little suite for voice and orchestra, *Faune et Bergère*, on three poems by Pushkin in the manner of Parny. Rimsky-Korsakov, who had closely followed the composition of these two works, wishing to give me the opportunity of hearing them, arranged with the Court orchestra to have them performed in the spring of 1907 at a private audition under the direction of its usual conductor H. Wahrlich.

In the season of 1907–1908, *Faune et Bergère* was given in public at one of the Belaieff concerts, conducted, if I remember rightly, by Felix Blumenfeld. I had two important works in hand at the same time: the *Scherzo Fantastique* and the first act of my opera, *Le Rossignol*, the libretto of which I had written in collaboration with my friend Mitoussov. It was based on a story by Hans Andersen. This work was greatly encouraged by my master, and to this day I remember with pleasure his approval of the preliminary sketches of these compositions. It grieves me much that he was never to hear them in their finished form, for I think that he would have liked them. Concurrently with this important work, I was composing two vocal settings for the words of a young Russian poet, Gorodetsky. He was one of a group of authors who, by their talent and their freshness, were destined to put new life into our somewhat old-fashioned poetry. These two songs were later called in French *La Novice* and *Sainte Rosée*. They and *Pastorale*, a song without words, were given at the Soirees in the winter of 1908. *Rimsky*

It was during that winter that my poor master's health began to fail. Frequent attacks of angina gave warning that it was only too likely that the end was near. I often went to see him, apart from my lessons, and he seemed to like my visits. He had my deep affection, and I was genuinely attached to him. It seems that these sentiments were reciprocated, but it was only later that I learned so from his family. His characteristic reserve had never allowed him to make any sort of display of his feelings.

Before starting for the country, where I generally spent vacation, my wife and I went to say good-by to him. That was the last time I saw him. In my talk with him I told him about a short orchestral fantasy, called *Feu d'Artifice*, that

I contemplated. He seemed interested, and told me to send it to him as soon as it was ready. I set to work as soon as I arrived at Oustilong, our estate in Volhynia, with the intention of sending the score to him for his daughter's wedding, which was shortly to take place. I finished it in six weeks and sent it off to the country place where he was spending the summer. A few days later a telegram informed me of his death, and shortly afterwards my registered packet was returned to me: "Not delivered on account of death of addressee." I joined his family at once in order to attend the funeral, which took place in St. Petersburg. The service was held in the chapel of the Conservatoire. His tomb, in the Novodievitchy Cemetery, is near that of my father.

On returning to the country, and wishing to pay some tribute to the memory of my master, I composed a *Chant Funèbre*, which was performed in the autumn, Felix Blumenfeld conducting, at the first Belaieff concert, which was dedicated to the memory of the great musician. The score of this work unfortunately disappeared in Russia during the Revolution, along with many other things which I had left there. I can no longer remember the music, but I can remember the idea at the root of its conception, which was that all the solo instruments of the orchestra filed past the tomb of the master in succession, each laying down its own melody as its wreath against a deep background of tremolo murmurings simulating the vibrations of bass voices singing in chorus. The impression made on the public, as well as on myself, was marked, but how far it was due to the atmosphere of mourning and how far to the merits of the composition itself I am no longer able to judge.

The presentation of the *Scherzo Fantastique* and *Feu d'Artifice* at the Siloti concerts in the winter marks a date of importance for the whole future of my musical career.

It was at this point that I began the close relations with Diaghileff which lasted for twenty years, right up to his death, and developed into a deep friendship based on a reciprocal affection that was proof against the difference of views or tastes which could not but arise from time to time in such a long period. Having heard the two compositions just mentioned, he commissioned me, among certain other Russian composers, to orchestrate two pieces by Chopin for the ballet, *Les Sylphides*, to be given in Paris in the spring of 1909. They were the *Nocturne* with which the dancing begins and the *Valse Brillante* with which the ballet closes. I could not go abroad that year, so that it was not until twelve months afterwards that I first heard my music in Paris.

These compositions, together with the death of Rimsky-Korsakov, had interrupted my work on the first act of my opera, *Le Rossignol*. In the summer of 1909 I returned to it with the firm intention of finishing it. There were to be three acts. But circumstances once again proved too strong for me. By the end of the summer the orchestration of the first act was finished, and, on returning to town, I meant to go on with the rest. But a telegram then arrived to upset all my plans. Diaghileff, who had just reached St. Petersburg, asked me to write the music for *L'Oiseau de Feu* for the Russian Ballet season at the Paris Opera House in the spring of 1910. Although alarmed by the fact that this was a commission for a fixed date, and afraid lest I should fail to complete the work in time – I was still unaware of my own capabilities – I accepted the order. It was highly flattering to be chosen from among the musicians of my generation, and to be allowed to collaborate in so important an enterprise side by side with personages who were generally recognized as masters in their own spheres.

Here I must interrupt the chronological sequence of my

story in order to give the reader a short account of the place which the ballet and ballet music occupied in intellectual circles and among so-called "serious" musicians in the period immediately preceding the appearance of the Diaghileff group. Although our ballet shone then, as always, by reason of its technical perfection, and although it filled the theatre, it was only rarely that these circles were represented among the audience. They considered this form of art as an inferior one, especially as compared with opera, which, though mishandled and turned into musical drama (which is not at all the same thing), still retained its own prestige. This was particularly the point of view in regard to the music of the classical ballet, which contemporary opinion considered to be unworthy of a serious composer. These poor souls had forgotten Glinka and his splendid dances in the Italian style in *Ruslan and Ludmilla*. It is true that Rimsky-Korsakov appreciated them – or, rather, forgave Glinka for them – but he himself, in his numerous operas, definitely gave the preference to character or national dances. We must not forget that it was these very pages of Glinka which inspired the great Russian composer, who was the first to bring about the serious recognition of ballet music in general – I refer to Tchaikovsky. In the early eighties he had had the audacity to compose a ballet for the Grand Theatre in Moscow, *Le Lac des Cygnes*, and he had to pay for his audacity by complete failure with the ignorant public, which would only admit ballet music as subsidiary and unimportant. His lack of success, however, did not prevent the Director of the Imperial Theatres, Ivan Vsevolojsky – a very enlightened and cultured aristocrat – from commissioning Tchaikovsky to compose another ballet, *The Sleeping Beauty*. It was produced with unprecedented lavishness (the production cost eighty thousand rubles) in the presence of the Emperor Alexander III at the Marie Theatre in St. Petersburg in December, 1889. This music was as much discussed by the incorrigible "balletomaniacs" as by the critics. They considered that it was too symphonic, and did not lend itself sufficiently to dancing. Nevertheless, it made a great impression on musicians, and completely changed their attitude towards the ballet in general. Thus, a few years later we see, one after the other, such composers as Glazounov, Arensky, and Tcherepnin composing ballets for the Imperial Theatres.

At the moment when I received Diaghileff's commission, the ballet had just undergone a great transformation owing to the advent of a young ballet master, Fokine, and the flowering of a whole bouquet of artists full of talent and originality: Pavlova, Karsavina, Nijinsky. Notwithstanding all my admiration for the classical ballet and its great master, Marius Petipa, I could not resist the intoxication produced by such ballets as *Les Danses du Prince Igor* or *Carnaval*, the only two of Fokine's productions that I had so far seen. All this greatly tempted me, and impelled me to break through the pale and eagerly seize this opportunity of making close contact with that group of advanced and active artists of which Diaghileff was the soul, and which had long attracted me.

Throughout the winter I worked strenuously at my ballet, and that brought me into constant touch with Diaghileff and his collaborators. Fokine created the choreography of *L'Oiseau de Feu* section by section, as the music was handed to him. I attended every rehearsal with the company, and after rehearsals Diaghileff, Nijinsky (who was, however, not dancing in the ballet), and myself generally ended the day with a fine dinner, washed down with good claret.

I then had an opportunity of observing Nijinsky at close

27

quarters. He spoke little, and, when he did speak, gave the impression of being a very backward youth, whose intelligence was very undeveloped for his age. But, whenever this occurred, Diaghileff, who was always beside him, would intervene and correct him so tactfully that no one noticed his embarrassing defects. I shall have further occasion to speak of Nijinsky when describing the part he took in my other ballets, either as dancer or choreographer.

Here I must say more of Diaghileff, because the close association I had with him during this first collaboration revealed the very essence of his great personality. What struck me most was the degree of endurance and tenacity that he displayed in pursuit of his ends. His strength in this direction was so exceptional that it was always somewhat terrifying, though at the same time reassuring, to work with him. It was terrifying because whenever there was a divergence of opinion it was arduous and exhausting to struggle with him. But it was reassuring to know that the goal was certain to be reached when once our differences had been overcome.

The quality of his intelligence and mentality also attracted me. He had a wonderful flair, a marvelous faculty for seizing at a glance the novelty and freshness of an idea, surrendering himself to it without pausing to reason it out. I do not mean to imply that he was at all lacking in reasoning power. On the contrary, his reasoning powers were unerring, and he had a most rational mind; and, though he frequently made mistakes or acted foolishly, it was because he had been carried away by passion or temperament – the two forces predominant in him.

He had at the same time a broad and generous nature, usually incapable of calculation, and, when he did calculate, it meant only that he himself was penniless. On the other hand, when he was in funds he spent lavishly on himself and on others. An odd trait in his character was his strange indifference towards the somewhat dubious honesty of some of those who were in touch with him – even when they victimized him – so long as their dishonesty was offset by other qualities. What he most detested were the commonplace, incapacity, a lack of *savoir faire*: he hated and despised a fool. Strangely enough, in this highly intelligent man, efficiency and shrewdness were accompanied by a certain childish ingenuousness. He never bore a grudge. When anyone swindled him, he was not angry, but would remark simply, "Well, what of it? He's looking after himself."

But to return to my score of *L'Oiseau de Feu*; I worked strenuously at it, and when I finished it on time I felt the need of a rest in the country before going to Paris, which I was to visit for the first time.

Diaghileff, with his company and collaborators, preceded me, so that when I joined them rehearsals were in full swing. Fokine elaborated the scenario, having worked at his choreography with burning devotion, the more so because he had fallen in love with the Russian fairy story. The casting was not what I had intended. Pavlova, with her slim angular figure, had seemed to me infinitely better suited to the role of the fairy bird than Karsavina, with her gentle feminine charm, for whom I had intended the part of the captive princess. Though circumstances had decided otherwise than I had planned, I had no cause for complaint, since Karsavina's rendering of the bird's part was perfect, and that beautiful and gracious artist had a brilliant success in it.

The performance was warmly applauded by the Paris public. I am, of course, far from attributing this success solely to the score; it was equally due to the spectacle on the stage

29

in the painter Golovin's magnificent setting, the brilliant interpretation by Diaghileff's artists, and the talent of the choreographer. I must admit, however, that the choreography of this ballet always seemed to me to be complicated and overburdened with plastic detail, so that the artists felt, and still feel even now, great difficulty in coordinating their steps and gestures with the music, and this often led to an unpleasant discordance between the movements of the dance and the imperative demands that the measure of the music imposed.

Although the evolution of the classical dance and its problems now seem much more real to me, and touch me more closely than the distant aesthetics of Fokine, I still consider that I have a right to form and express the opinion that in the sphere of choreography I prefer, for example, the vigor of the *Danses du Prince Igor*, with their clear-cut and positive lines, to the somewhat detached designs of *L'Oiseau de Feu*.

Returning for a moment to the music, it gives me much pleasure to pay grateful tribute to the mastery with which the eminent Gabriel Pierné conducted my work.

While I was in Paris I had the opportunity of meeting several persons of importance in the world of music, such as Debussy, Ravel, Florent Schmitt, and Manuel de Falla, who were there at that time. I recall that on the first night Debussy came on to the stage and complimented me on my score. That was the beginning of friendly relations which lasted to the end of his life.

The approbation, and even admiration, extended to me by the artistic and musical world in general, but more particularly by representatives of the younger generation, greatly strengthened me in regard to the plans which I had in mind for the future — I am thinking in particular of *Petroushka*, of which I shall have more to say later.

One day, when I was finishing the last pages of *L'Oiseau de Feu* in St. Petersburg, I had a fleeting vision which came to me as a complete surprise, my mind at the moment being full of other things. I saw in imagination a solemn pagan rite: sage elders, seated in a circle, watched a young girl dance herself to death. They were sacrificing her to propitiate the god of spring. Such was the theme of the *Sacre du Printemps*. I must confess that this vision made a deep impression on me, and I at once described it to my friend, Nicholas Roerich, he being a painter who had specialized in pagan subjects. He welcomed my inspiration with enthusiasm, and became my collaborator in this creation. In Paris I told Diaghileff about it, and he was at once carried away by the idea, though its realization was delayed by the following events.

At the end of the Paris season I had a short rest at the sea, in which I composed two songs to Verlaine's words, and at the end of August I went to Switzerland with my family.

Before tackling the Sacre du Printemps, which would be a long and difficult task, I wanted to refresh myself by composing an orchestral piece in which the piano would play the most important part — a sort of *Konzertstück*. In composing the music, I had in my mind a distinct picture of a puppet, suddenly endowed with life, exasperating the patience of the orchestra with diabolical cascades of arpeggios. The orchestra in turn retaliates with menacing trumpet blasts. The outcome is a terrific noise which reaches its climax and ends in the sorrowful and querulous collapse of the poor puppet. Having finished this bizarre piece, I struggled for hours, while walking beside the Lake of Geneva, to find a title which would express in a word the character of my

31

music and, consequently, the personality of this creature.

One day I leapt for joy. I had indeed found my title –
Petroushka, the immortal and unhappy hero of every fair in
all countries. Soon afterwards Diaghileff came to visit me at
Clarens, where I was staying. He was much astonished when,
instead of sketches of the *Sacre*, I played him the piece I had
just composed and which later became the second scene of
Petroushka. He was so much pleased with it that he would
not leave it alone and began persuading me to develop the
theme of the puppet's sufferings and make it into a whole
ballet. While he remained in Switzerland we worked out
together the general lines of the subject and the plot in accordance with ideas which I suggested. We settled the scene
of action: the fair, with its crowd, its booths, the little traditional theatre, the character of the magician, with all his
tricks; and the coming to life of the dolls – *Petroushka*, his
rival, and the dancer – and their love tragedy, which ends
with Petroushka's death. I began at once to compose the
first scene of the ballet, which I finished at Beaulieu, where
I spent the winter with my family. While there, I frequently
saw Diaghileff, who was at Monte Carlo. By mutual agreement, Diaghileff entrusted the whole *décor* of the ballet,
both the scenery and the costumes, to Benois. Diaghileff
soon went off to St. Petersburg, whence he wrote at Christmas, asking me to join him there for a few days, bringing my
music so that Benois and his other collaborators might see it.
I went in some trepidation. The suddenness of the transition
from the sunny warmth of Beaulieu to the fog and snow of
my native city struck me with great force.

As soon as I arrived I let my friends hear what I had so
far composed for *Petroushka* – namely, the first two scenes
and the beginning of the third. Benois immediately began

work, and in the spring he joined us at Monte Carlo, whither Diaghileff and I had returned.

I little thought then that I had seen my native town for the last time – St. Petersburg, the town of St. Peter, dedicated by Peter the Great to his great patron saint and not to himself, as was doubtless supposed by the ignorant inventors of the absurd name, Petrograd.

When I returned to Beaulieu, I resumed work on my score, but its progress was interrupted. I became seriously ill with nicotine poisoning, and was at the point of death, this illness causing a month of enforced idleness. I was terribly anxious about the fate of *Petroushka*, which had at all costs to be ready for Paris in the spring. Fortunately I recovered my strength sufficiently to enable me to finish my work in the ten weeks which remained before the beginning of the season. Towards the end of April I set out for Rome, where Diaghileff was giving performances at the Costanzi Theatre during the International Exhibition. There *Petroushka* was rehearsed, and there I finished its last pages.

I shall always remember with particular pleasure that spring in Rome, which I was seeing for the first time. I stayed at the Albergo d'Italia with Benois and the Russian painter, Serov, to whom I became greatly attached. In spite of my strenuous work, we found time to make various expeditions which were very instructive for me, as Benois was a learned connoisseur in matters of art and history and had a talent for making the past live, so that these expeditions provided a veritable education in which I delighted.

On our arrival in Paris, rehearsals started under the direction of Pierre Monteux, who was for several years the conductor of the Russian Ballet. From an instrumentalist in Colonne's orchestra he had attained the rank of assistant conductor. He knew his job thoroughly, and was so familiar with the surroundings from which he had risen that he knew how to get on with his musicians – a great asset for a conductor. Thus he was able to achieve a very clean and finished execution of my score. I ask no more of a conductor, for any other attitude on his part immediately turns into *interpretation*, a thing I have a horror of. The *interpreter* of necessity can think of nothing but *interpretation*, and thus takes on the garb of a translator, *traduttore-traditore*; this is an absurdity in music, and for the interpreter it is a source of vanity inevitably leading to the most ridiculous megalomania. During the rehearsals I had the great satisfaction of seeing that all my intentions with regard to sound effects were amply confirmed.

At the dress rehearsal at the Chatelet, to which the Press and the elite of the artistic world had been invited, I remember the *Petroushka* produced an immediate effect on everyone in the audience with the exception of a few hypercritics. One of them – it is true that he was a literary critic – actually went up to Diaghileff and said: "And it was to hear this that you invited us!" "Exactly," replied Diaghileff. It is only fair to add that later on the celebrated critic, to judge by his praise, seemed to have forgotten this sally.

I should like at this point to pay heartfelt homage to Vaslav Nijinsky's unsurpassed rendering of the role of Petroushka. The perfection with which he became the very incarnation of this character was all the more remarkable because the purely saltatory work in which he usually excelled was in this case definitely dominated by dramatic action, music, and gesture. The beauty of the ballet was greatly enhanced by the richness of the artistic setting that Benois had created for it. My faithful interpreter, Karsavina,

34

swore to me that she would never relinquish her part as the dancer, which she adored. But it was a pity that the movements of the crowd had been neglected. I mean that they were left to the arbitrary improvisation of the performers instead of being choreographically regulated in accordance with the clearly defined exigencies of the music. I regret it all the more because the *danses d'ensemble* of the coachmen, nurses, and mummers and the solo dances must be regarded as Fokine's finest creations.

As for my present opinion of the music of *Petroushka*, I think it will be best to refer the reader to the pages that I shall devote later to my own rendering of my works, which will necessarily lead me to speak of them.

And now for the *Sacre du Printemps*.

As I have already said, when I conceived the idea, immediately after *L'Oiseau de Feu*, I became so much absorbed in the composition of *Petroushka* that I had no chance even to sketch preliminary outlines.

After the Paris season, I returned to Oustiloug, our estate in Russia, to devote myself entirely to the *Sacre du Printemps*. I found time, however, to compose two melodies to the words of the Russian poet Balmont. Besides that, also to Balmont's words, I composed a cantata for choir and orchestra, *Zvezdoliki* (The King of the Stars), which I dedicated to Claude Debussy. Owing, however, to inherent difficulties involved in the execution of this very short piece, with its important orchestral contingent and the complexity of its choral writing as regards intonation, it has never been performed.

Although I had conceived the subject of the *Sacre du Printemps* without any plot, some plan had to be designed for the sacrificial action. For this it was necessary that I

should see Roerich. He was staying at the moment at Talach-
kino, the estate of Princess Tenicheva, a great patron of
Russian art. I joined him, and it was there that we settled
the visual embodiment of the *Sacre* and the definite sequence
of its different episodes. I began the score on returning to
Oustiloug, and worked at it through the winter at Clarens.

Diaghileff made up his mind that year that he would
spare no effort to make a choreographer of Nijinsky. I do not
know whether he really believed in his choreographic gifts,
or whether he thought that his talented dancing, about
which he raved, indicated that he would show equal talent
as a ballet master. However that may be, his idea was to make
Nijinsky compose, under his own strict supervision, a sort of
antique tableau conjuring up the erotic gambols of a faun
importuning nymphs. At the suggestion of Bakst, who was
obsessed by ancient Greece, this tableau was to be presented
as an animated bas-relief, with the figures in profile. Bakst
dominated this production. Besides creating the decorative
setting and the beautiful costumes, he inspired the choreography even to the slightest movements. Nothing better could
be found for this ballet than the impressionist music of Debussy, who, however, evinced little enthusiasm for the project. Diaghileff nevertheless, by dint of his persistence, wrung
a half-hearted consent from him, and, after repeated and
laborious rehearsals, the ballet was set afoot and was produced in Paris in the spring. The scandal which it produced
is a matter of history, but that scandal was in nowise due to
the so-called novelty of the performance, but to a gesture,
too audacious and too intimate, which Nijinsky made, doubtless thinking that anything was permissible with an erotic
subject and perhaps wishing thereby to enhance the effect
of the production. I mention this only because it was so much

discussed at the time. At this date the aesthetics and the whole spirit of this kind of scenic display seem so stale that I have not the least desire to discuss them further.

Nijinsky had been so busily engaged in making his first attempts as ballet master, and in studying new roles, that he obviously had had neither time nor strength to deal with the *Sacre du Printemps*, the choreography of which had been entrusted to him. Fokine was occupied with other ballets – Ravel's *Daphnis et Chloé* and Reynaldo Hahn's *Le Dieu Bleu*. The production of the *Sacre*, the score of which I had meanwhile finished, had therefore to be put off till the following year. This allowed me to take a rest and to work without haste on the orchestration.

When I returned to Paris for the Diaghileff season, I heard, among other things, the brilliant score of Maurice Ravel's *Daphnis et Chloé*, Ravel having previously given me some idea of it by playing it to me on the piano. Not only is it one of Ravel's greatest achievements, it is one of the finest things in French music. If I am not mistaken it was in that year, while seated, by Debussy's invitation, in his box at the Opéra Comique, that I heard for the first time another great French work, *Pelléas et Mélisande*. I was seeing a good deal of Debussy, and was deeply touched by his sympathetic attitude towards me and my music. I was struck by the delicacy of his appreciation, and was grateful to him, among other things, for having observed what so few had then noticed – the musical importance of the pages which precede the juggling tricks in *Petroushka* immediately before the final dance of the marionettes in the first act. Debussy often invited me to his house, and on one occasion I met there Erik Satie, whom I already knew by name. I liked him at once. He was a quick-witted fellow, shrewd, clever, and mordant. Of his

37

compositions I prefer above all his *Socrate* and certain pages of his *Parade*.

From Paris I went as usual to Oustiloug for the summer, and there I quietly continued my work on the *Sacre*. I was roused from that peaceful existence by an invitation from Diaghileff to join him at Bayreuth to hear *Parsifal* in its hallowed setting. I had never seen *Parsifal* on the stage. The proposal was tempting, and I accepted it with pleasure. On the way I stopped at Nuremberg for twenty-four hours and visited the museum. Next day my dear, portly friend met me at the Bayreuth station and told me that we were in danger of having to sleep in the open, as all the hotels were filled to overflowing. We managed, however, with great difficulty, to find two servants' rooms. The performance that I saw there would not tempt me today, even if I were offered a room gratis. The very atmosphere of the theatre, its design and its setting, seemed lugubrious. It was like a crematorium, and a very old-fashioned one at that, and one expected to see the gentleman in black who had been entrusted with the task of singing the praises of the departed. The order to devote oneself to contemplation was given by a blast of trumpets. I sat humble and motionless, but at the end of a quarter of an hour I could bear no more. My limbs were numb and I had to change my position. Crack! Now I had done it! My chair had made a noise which drew down on me the furious scowls of a hundred pairs of eyes. Once more I withdrew into myself, but I could think of only one thing, and that was the end of the act which would put an end to my martyrdom. At last the intermission arrived, and I was rewarded by two sausages and a glass of beer. But hardly had I had time to light a cigarette when the trumpet blast sounded again, demanding another period of contemplation. Another act to be got through, when all my thoughts were concentrated on my cigarette, of which I had had barely a whiff. I managed to bear the second act. Then there were more sausages, more beer, another trumpet blast, another period of contemplation, another act – finis!

I do not want to discuss the music of *Parsifal* or the music of Wagner in general. At this date it is too remote from me. What I find revolting in the whole affair is the underlying conception which dictated it – the principle of putting a work of art on the same level as the sacred and symbolic ritual which constitutes a religious service. And, indeed, is not all this comedy of Bayreuth, with its ridiculous formalities, simply an unconscious aping of a religious rite?

Perhaps someone may cite the mysteries of the Middle Ages in contravention of this view. But those performances had religion as their basis and faith as their source. The spirit of the mystery plays did not venture beyond the bosom of the Church which patronized them. They were religious ceremonies bordering on the canonical rites, and such aesthetic qualities as they might contain were merely accessory and unintentional, and in no way affected their substance. Such ceremonies were due to the imperious desire of the faithful to see the objects of their faith incarnate and in palpable form – the same desire as that which created statues and ikons in the churches.

It is high time to put an end, once and for all, to this unseemly and sacrilegious conception of art as religion and the theatre as a temple. The following argument will readily show the absurdity of such pitiful aesthetics: one cannot imagine a believer adopting a critical attitude towards a religious service. That would be a contradiction in terms; the believer would cease to be a believer. The attitude of an audience is exactly the opposite. It is not dependent upon faith or blind submission. At a performance one admires or one rejects. One accepts only after having passed judgment, however little one may be aware of it. The critical faculty plays an essential part. To confound these two distinct lines of thought is to give proof of a complete lack of discernment, and certainly of bad taste. But is it at all surprising that such confusion should arise at a time like the present, when the openly irreligious masses in their degradation of spiritual values and debasement of human thought necessarily lead us to utter brutalization? People are, however, apparently fully aware of the sort of monster to which the world is about to give birth, and perceive with annoyance that man cannot live without some kind of cult. An effort is therefore made to refurbish old cults dragged from some revolutionary arsenal, wherewith to enter into competition with the Church.

But to return to the *Sacre*. To be perfectly frank, I must say here and now that the idea of working with Nijinsky filled me with misgiving, notwithstanding our friendliness and my great admiration for his talent as dancer and mime. His ignorance of the most elementary notions of music was flagrant. The poor boy knew nothing of music. He could neither read it nor play any instrument, and his reactions to music were expressed in banal phrases or the repetition of what he had heard others say. As one was unable to discover any individual impressions, one began to doubt whether he had any. These lacunae were so serious that his plastic vision, often of great beauty, could not compensate for them. My apprehensions can be readily understood, but I had no choice in the matter. Fokine had dissociated himself from Diaghileff, and in any case, considering his aesthetic tendencies, he would doubtless have refused to work at the *Sacre*; Romanov

40

was busy with Florent Schmitt's *Salomé*; only Nijinsky remained, and Diaghileff, still hopeful of making a ballet master of him, insisted that he should put on both the *Sacre* and Debussy's *Jeux*.

Nijinsky began by demanding such a fantastic number of rehearsals that it was physically impossible to give them to him. It will not be difficult to understand why he wanted so many, when I say that in trying to explain to him the construction of my work in general outline and in detail I discovered that I should achieve nothing until I had taught him the very rudiments of music: values — semibreve, minim, crochet, quaver, etc. — bars, rhythm, tempo, and so on. He had the greatest difficulty in remembering any of this. Nor was that all. When, in listening to music, he contemplated movements, it was always necessary to remind him that he must make them accord with the tempo, its divisions and values. It was exasperating and we advanced at a snail's pace. It was all the more trying because Nijinsky complicated and encumbered his dances beyond all reason, thus creating difficulties for the dancers that were sometimes impossible to overcome. This was due as much to his lack of experience as to the complexity of a task with which he was unfamiliar.

Under these conditions I did not want to leave him to his own devices, partly because of my kindly feeling for him but partly on account of my work and considerations as to its fate. I therefore traveled a great deal so as to attend the rehearsals of the company, which, throughout that winter, took place in the different towns in which Diaghileff was giving performances. The atmosphere was always heavy and stormy. It was evident that the poor boy had been saddled with a task beyond his capacity.

He appeared to be quite unconscious both of his inadequacy and of the fact that he had been given a role which, to put it shortly, he was incapable of filling in so serious an undertaking as the Russian Ballet. Seeing that he was losing prestige with the company but was strongly upheld by Diaghileff, he became presumptuous, capricious, and unmanageable. The natural result was a series of painful incidents which seriously complicated matters.

It should not be necessary for me to emphasize that in writing all this I have not the least desire to cast any slur on the fame of this magnificent artist. We were, as I have already said, always on the best of terms, and I have never ceased to admire his great talent for dancing and mime. He will always live in my memory, and I hope in the memory of everyone who had the good fortune to see him dance, as one of the most beautiful visions that ever appeared on the stage.

But now that this great artist is, alas! the victim of mental malady, his name belongs to history, and I should be false to history if, in assessing his worth as an artist, I perpetuated the confusion which has arisen between his work as interpreter and as creator. From what I have said above it should be obvious that Diaghileff himself is mainly responsible for that confusion, though that does not in any way detract from my feeling of deep admiration for my great departed friend. It is true that I refrained at the time from telling Nijinsky what I thought of his efforts as a ballet master. I did not like to do so. I had to spare his self-respect, and I knew in advance that his mentality and character would make any such conversation alike painful and useless. On the other hand, I had no hesitation in often talking about it to Diaghileff. He, however, persisted in pushing Nijinsky along that path, either because he regarded the gift of plastic vision as the most important factor in choreographic art, or because he kept on hoping that the qualities which seemed lacking in Nijinsky would one day or another suddenly manifest themselves.

I worked continuously at the score of the *Sacre* at Clarens throughout the winter of 1912–1913, my work being interrupted only by interviews with Diaghileff, who invited me to the first performances of *L'Oiseau de Feu* and *Petroushka* in the different towns of central Europe where the Russian Ballet was on tour.

My first journey was to Berlin. I very well remember the performance before the Kaiser, the Kaiserin, and their suite. The program consisted of *Cléopâtre* and *Petroushka*. The Kaiser naturally gave preference to *Cléopâtre*, and, in complimenting Diaghileff, told him that he would send his Egyptologists to see the ballet and take a lesson from it. He apparently thought that Bakst's fantastic coloring was a scrupulously historical reproduction, and that the potpourri of the score was a revelation of ancient Egyptian music. At another performance, when *L'Oiseau de Feu* was given, I made the acquaintance of Richard Strauss, who came on to the stage and expressed great interest in the music. Among other things, he said something which much amused me: "You make a mistake in beginning your piece *pianissimo*; the public will not listen. You should astonish them by a sudden crash at the very start. After that they will follow you and you can do whatever you like."

It was on that visit to Berlin that I first met Schönberg, who invited me to an audition of his *Pierrot Lunaire*. I did not feel the slightest enthusiasm about the aesthetics of the work, which appeared to me to be a retrogression to the out-of-date Beardsley cult. But, on the other hand, I consider

43

(that the merits of the instrumentation are beyond dispute.

Budapest, the next town we visited, made a very agreeable impression on me. Its inhabitants are very open-hearted, warm and kindly. Everything went well there, and my ballets, *L'Oiseau de Feu* and *Petroushka*, had an enormous success. When I visited the town many years later I was greatly moved at being received by the public as an old friend. It was quite the reverse in Vienna, of which I retain a somewhat bitter memory. The hostility with which the orchestra received the music of *Petroushka* at rehearsal greatly astonished me. I had not come across anything like it in any country. I admit that at that time an orchestra as conservative as that in Vienna might have failed to grasp parts of my music, but I was far from expecting that its hostility would be carried to the length of open sabotage at rehearsals and the audible utterance of such coarse remarks as "*schmutzige Musik.*" The entire administration shared this aversion, which was aimed particularly at the Prussian comptroller of the Hofoper, for it was he who had engaged Diaghileff and his company and thereby roused the furious jealousy of the Imperial Ballet of Vienna. I ought to add that Russians were not very popular in Austria just then by reason of the somewhat strained political situation. Still, in spite of the old-fashioned tastes and habits of the Viennese, the performance of *Petroushka* passed without protest, and even had a certain success. I was astonished to find a comforter in the person of a workman whose job it was to lower and raise the curtain. Seeing that I was upset by my trouble with the orchestra, this friendly old man, bewhiskered in the style of Franz Joseph, patted my shoulder kindly and said: "Don't let's be downhearted. I've been here for fifty-five years, and it's not the first time that things of that sort have happened. It was just the same with *Tristan*." I shall have something more to say about Vienna later, but for the moment let us return to Clarens.

While putting the finishing touches to the orchestration of the *Sacre*, I was busy with another composition which was very close to my heart. In the summer I had read a little anthology of Japanese lyrics – short poems of a few lines each, selected from the old poets. The impression which they had made on me was exactly like that made by Japanese paintings and engravings. The graphic solution of problems of perspective and space shown by their art incited me to find something analogous in music. Nothing could have lent itself better to this than the Russian version of the Japanese poems, owing to the well-known fact that Russian verse allows the tonic accent only. I gave myself up to the task, and succeeded by a metrical and rhythmic process too complex to be explained here.

Towards the end of the winter, Diaghileff gave me another commission. He had decided to give Moussorgsky's *Khovanstchina* in the next Paris season. This opera, as everybody knows, had not been quite finished by the composer, and Diaghileff asked me to take it in hand. Rimsky-Korsakov had already arranged it in his own manner, and it was in his version that it had been published and performed in Russia.

Diaghileff was not satisfied with Rimsky-Korsakov's general treatment of Moussorgsky's work, and began to study the original manuscript of *Khovanstchina* with a view to making a new version. He asked me to undertake the orchestration of such parts as had not been orchestrated by the author, and to compose a chorus for the finale, for which Moussorgsky had indicated only the theme – an authentic Russian song.

45

When I saw how much there was to be done, and still having to finish the score of the *Sacre*, I asked Diaghileff to divide the work between myself and Ravel. He willingly consented to this, and Ravel joined me at Clarens so that we might work together. We agreed that I should orchestrate two parts of the opera and write the final chorus, while he undertook the rest. According to Diaghileff's plan, our work was to be amalgamated with the rest of the score, but unfortunately it made the mixture even more incongruously heterogeneous than Rimsky-Korsakov's version, which had been retained in all essentials, the only difference being a few cuts, a change in the order of certain scenes, and the substitution of my chorus for his. Apart from the work mentioned above, I had no share in the arrangement of this version. I have always been sincerely opposed to the rearrangement by anyone other than the author himself of work already created, and my opposition is only strengthened when the original author is an artist as conscious and certain of what he was doing as Moussorgsky. To my mind that principle is as badly violated in the Diaghileff compilation as it was in Rimsky-Korsakov's Meyerbeerization of *Boris Godounov*.

While Ravel was at Clarens I played him my Japanese poems. An epicure and connoisseur of instrumental jewelry, and quick to discern the subtleties of writing, he grasped the idea at once and decided to do something similar. Soon afterwards he played me his delicious *Poèmes de Mallarmé*.

I have now come to the spring season of 1913 in Paris, when the Russian Ballet inaugurated the opening of the Théatre des Champs-Elysées. It began with a revival of *L'Oiseau de Feu*, and the *Sacre du Printemps* was given on May 28 at the evening performance. The complexity of my score had demanded a great number of rehearsals, which Monteux had conducted with his usual skill and attention. As for the actual performance, I am not in a position to judge, as I left the auditorium at the first bars of the prelude, which had at once evoked derisive laughter. I was disgusted. These demonstrations, at first isolated, soon became general, provoking counter-demonstrations and very quickly developing into a terrific uproar. During the whole performance I was at Nijinsky's side in the wings. He was standing on a chair, screaming "sixteen, seventeen, eighteen" – they had their own method of counting to keep time. Naturally the poor dancers could hear nothing by reason of the row in the auditorium and the sound of their own dance steps. I had to hold Nijinsky by his clothes, for he was furious, and ready to dash on to the stage at any moment and create a scandal. Diaghileff kept ordering the electricians to turn the lights on or off, hoping in that way to put a stop to the noise. That is all I can remember about that first performance. Oddly enough, at the dress rehearsal, to which we had, as usual, invited a number of actors, painters, musicians, writers, and the most cultured representatives of society, everything had gone off peacefully, and I was very far from expecting such an outburst.

Now, after the lapse of more than twenty years, it is naturally difficult for me to recall in any detail the choreography of the *Sacre* without being influenced by the admiration with which it met in the set known as the *avant-garde* – ready, as always, to welcome as a new discovery anything that differs, be it ever so little, from the *déjà vu*. But what struck me then, and still strikes me most, about the choreography, was and is Nijinsky's lack of consciousness of what he was doing in creating it. He showed therein his complete inability to accept and assimilate those revolutionary ideas which Diaghileff had made his creed, and obstinately and industriously strove to inculcate. What the choreography expressed was a very labored and barren effort rather than a plastic realization flowing simply and naturally from what the music demanded. How far it all was from what I had desired!

In composing the *Sacre* I had imagined the spectacular part of the performance as a series of rhythmic mass movements of the greatest simplicity which would have an instantaneous effect on the audience, with no superfluous details or complications such as would suggest effort. The only solo was to be the sacrificial dance at the end of the piece. The music of that dance, clear and well defined, demanded a corresponding choreography – simple and easy to understand. But there again, although he had grasped the dramatic significance of the dance, Nijinsky was incapable of giving intelligible form to its essence, and complicated it either by clumsiness or lack of understanding. For it is undeniably clumsy to slow down the tempo of the music in order to compose complicated steps which cannot be danced in the tempo prescribed. Many choreographers have that fault, but I have never known any who erred in that respect to the same degree as Nijinsky.

In reading what I have written about the *Sacre*, the reader will perhaps be astonished to notice how little I have said about the music. The omission is deliberate. It is impossible, after the lapse of twenty years, to recall what were the feelings which animated me in composing it. One can recollect facts or incidents with more or less exactitude, but one cannot reconstitute feelings without the risk of distorting them under the influence of the many changes that one has meanwhile undergone. Any account I were to give today of what my feelings were at that time might prove as inexact and arbitrary as if someone else where interpreting them. It would be something like an interview with me unwarrantably signed with my name – something which has, alas! happened only too often.

One such incident comes to my mind in connection with this very production. Among the most assiduous onlookers at the rehearsals had been a certain Ricciotto Canuedo, a charming man, devoted to everything advanced and up to date. He was at that time publishing a review called *Montjoie*. When he asked me for an interview, I very willingly granted it. Unfortunately, it appeared in the form of a pronouncement on the *Sacre*, at once grandiloquent and naive, and, to my great astonishment, signed with my name. I could not recognize myself, and was much disturbed by this distortion of my language and even of my ideas, especially as the pronouncement was generally regarded as authentic, and the scandal over the *Sacre* had noticeably increased the sale of the review. But I was too ill at the time to be able to set things right.

I did not see the subsequent performances of the *Sacre*, nor could I go to see *Khovanstchina* because a few days after the notorious first night I fell ill with typhoid and spent six weeks in a nursing home.

As for Debussy's *Jeux*, I clearly remember having seen it, but I cannot be sure whether at the dress rehearsal or on the first night. I very much like the music, which Debussy had already played to me on the piano. How well that man played! The animation and vivacity of the score merited a warmer reception than it got from the public. My mind is a complete blank with regard to its choreography.

During the long weeks of my illness, I was the subject of the most lively and touching solicitude on the part of my friends. Debussy, De Falla, Ravel, Florent Schmitt, and Casella all came to see me frequently. Diaghileff called nearly every day, though he never came into my room, so great was his fear of contagion. This fear was almost pathological, and his friends often chaffed him about it. Maurice Delage was with me constantly. I was greatly attracted by his buoyant disposition, and I much appreciated the delicacy and penetration of his musical feeling, to which his compositions – alas! far too few in number – bear witness. He was also gifted in many other ways, so that he was very good company.

On returning to Oustiloug after my illness, I did not feel strong enough to undertake any important work, but, so that I should not be completely idle, amused myself with the composition of several small things. I recall writing during the summer three short pieces for voice and piano, called *Souvenirs de mon Enfance*, which I dedicated to my children. They were melodies that I had invented and had taken as themes for improvisation to amuse my companions in earlier years. I had always meant to give them a definite form, and took advantage of my leisure to do so. Some years ago (1923) I made another version of them for a small orchestral ensemble, amplifying them here and there in accordance with the orchestral requirements.

Hardly had I got back to Clarens, with the intention of spending the winter there as usual, when I received from the newly founded Théatre Libre of Moscow a request to complete the composition of my opera, *Le Rossignol*. I hesitated. Only the Prologue – that is to say, Act I – was in existence. It had been written four years earlier, and my musical language had been appreciably modified since then.

I feared that in view of my new manner the subsequent scenes would clash with that Prologue. I informed the directors of the Théatre Libre of my misgivings, and suggested that they should be content with the Prologue alone, presenting it as an independent little lyrical scene. But they insisted upon the entire opera in three acts, and ended by persuading me.

As there is no action until the second act, I told myself that it would not be unreasonable if the music of the Prologue bore a somewhat different character from that of the rest. And, indeed, the forest, with its nightingale, the pure soul of the child who falls in love with its song . . . all this gentle poetry of Hans Andersen's could not be expressed in the same way as the baroque luxury of the Chinese Court, with its bizarre etiquette, its palace fetes, its thousands of little bells and lanterns, and the grotesque humming of the mechanical Japanese nightingale . . . in short, all this exotic fantasy obviously demanded a different musical idiom.

I set to work, and it took me all the winter, but even before I had finished the score the news reached me that the whole enterprise of the Théatre Libre of Moscow had collapsed. I could, therefore, dispose of the opera as I liked, and Diaghileff, who had been chagrined to see me working for another theatre, jumped at the chance, and decided to put it on in his next season at the Paris Opera House. It was all the more easy for him because he was to produce Rimsky-Korsakov's *Le Coq d'Or*, and therefore already had the necessary singers. Benois created sumptuous scenery and costumes, and, conducted by Monteux, the opera was performed with the utmost perfection.

I must go back a little to mention something of great importance to me that happened before the Paris opera season. I think that it was in the month of April, 1914, that both the *Sacre* and *Petroushka* were played for the first time at a concert in Paris, Monteux being the conductor. It was a brilliant renaissance of the *Sacre* after the Théatre des Champs-Elysées scandal. The hall was crowded. The audience, with no scenery to distract them, listened with concentrated attention and applauded with an enthusiasm I had been far from expecting and which greatly moved me. Certain critics who had censured the *Sacre* the year before now openly admitted their mistake. This conquest of the public naturally gave me intense and lasting satisfaction.

About this time I made the acquaintance of Ernest Ansermet, conductor of the orchestra at Montreux, who lived at Clarens, quite close to me. A friendship quickly sprang up between us, and I remember that it was at one of his rehearsals that he suggested that I should take the baton and read my first symphony, which he had included in his program, with the orchestra. That was my first attempt at conducting.

On my return from Paris I settled in the mountains with my family at Salvan (Valais). But I soon had to run over to London to be present at the performance of *Le Rossignol*, which Diaghileff was producing this time, with Emile Cooper as conductor.

Back again at Salvan, I composed three pieces for string quartet which I had time to finish before going to make a short stay at Oustiloug and at Kiev. Meanwhile I had been thinking of a grand *divertissement*, or rather a cantata depicting peasant nuptials. Among the collections of Russian folk poems in Kiev I found many bearing on this subject, and made a selection from them which I took back with me to Switzerland.

52

On my way from Russia via Warsaw, Berlin, and Basle, I was very conscious of the tense atmosphere all over central Europe, and I felt certain that we were on the eve of serious events. A fortnight later war was declared. As I had been exempted from military service, there was no need for me to return to Russia, which, though I had no inkling of it, I was never to see again as I had known it.

IV

My profound emotion on reading the news of war, which aroused patriotic feelings and a sense of sadness at being so distant from my country, found some alleviation in the delight with which I steeped myself in Russian folk poems.

What fascinated me in this verse was not so much the stories, which were often crude, or the pictures and metaphors, always so deliciously unexpected, as the sequence of the words and syllables, and the cadence they create, which produces an effect on one's sensibilities very closely akin to that of music. For I consider that music is, by its very nature, essentially powerless to *express* anything at all, whether a feeling, an attitude of mind, a psychological mood, a phenomenon of nature, etc.... *Expression* has never been an inherent property of music. That is by no means the purpose of its existence. If, as is nearly always the case, music appears to express something, this is only an illusion and not a reality. It is simply an additional attribute which, by tacit and inveterate agreement, we have lent it, thrust upon it, as a label, a convention – in short, an aspect unconsciously or by force of habit, we have come to confuse with its essential being.

Music is the sole domain in which man realizes the present. By the imperfection of his nature, man is doomed to submit to the passage of time – to its categories of past and future – without ever being able to give substance, and therefore stability, to the category of the present.

The phenomenon of music is given to us with the sole purpose of establishing an order in things, including, and particularly, the coordination between *man* and *time*. To be put into practice, its indispensable and single requirement is construction. Construction once completed, this order has been attained, and there is nothing more to be said. It would be futile to look for, or expect anything else from it. It is precisely this construction, this achieved order, which produces in us a unique emotion having nothing in common with our ordinary sensations and our responses to the impressions of daily life. One could not better define the sensation produced by music than by saying that it is identical with that evoked by contemplation of the interplay of architectural forms. Goethe thoroughly understood that when he called architecture petrified music.

After this digression, which I felt it wise to interpolate at this point – but which far from exhausts my reflections on the subject, into which I shall have occasion to go more deeply – I come back to the Russian folk poems. I culled a bouquet from among them all, which I distributed in three different compositions that I wrote one after the other, elaborating my material for *Les Noces*. They were *Pribaoutki* (translated by Ramuz under the title *Chansons Plaisantes*), for voice, with the accompaniment of a small orchestra; then *Les Berceuses du Chat*, also for voice, accompanied by three clarinets; and, lastly, four little choruses for women's voices *a capella*.

In the autumn I returned to Clarens, where Ansermet – who had moved to Lausanne – sublet to me the little house that he had just left, and there I passed the winter of 1914–1915. I was working at *Les Noces* the whole time. Confined to Switzerland after the declaration of war, I formed there a little circle of friends, the chief of whom were C. F. Ramuz, the painter R. Auberjonois, the brothers Alexandre and Charles Albert Cingria, Ernest Ansermet, the brothers Jean and René Mora, Fernant Chavennes, and Henri Bischoff.

Our removal to the Vaud, where I lived for six years, began an important period, to which my great friend Ramuz has devoted a book, *Souvenirs sur Igor Stravinsky*. This volume, to which I refer those interested in that part of my life, testifies to our deep affection for each other, to those feelings which each of us found echoed in the other, to the attachment that we both had for his dear Vaud country that had brought us together, and to his deep and understanding sympathy.

Hardly had I settled at Clarens when I received a pressing appeal from Diaghileff to pay him a visit at Florence. He, like myself, was going through a very difficult time. The war had upset all his plans. The greater part of his company had dispersed, and it was necessary for him to arrange regroupings to enable him to carry on and support himself. In that painful situation he felt the need for having a friend at hand to console him, to encourage him, and to help him with advice.

My own situation was no better. I had to make all the arrangements for my mother's safe return to Russia – she had spent the summer with us – and for supplying the needs of my wife and four children; and, with the slender resources which one could get from Russia, the maintenance of the family became more and more difficult.

Nevertheless, I went to Florence, for I was as anxious as my friend to share the gloomy thoughts which obsessed us both. After spending a fortnight there, I returned to Clarens. But in the course of the winter, my wife's health, which had been greatly tried by her recent confinement, decided me to get her into mountain air, and, after closing our house at Clarens, we betook ourselves to Chateau d'Oex for about two months.

My stay there was broken by another journey to Rome, which I undertood in response to a new appeal from Diaghileff. It was just at the time of the terrible earthquake at Avezzano, the repercussions of which we felt even at Chateau d'Oex. In these circumstances I was a little perturbed at the thought of leaving my family to go into Italy, where everyone was still overshadowed by the catastrophe, and apprehensive of further shocks. All the same, I decided to make the journey.

Diaghileff had taken a furnished apartment in Rome for the winter, and I joined him there. In my luggage I had three little pieces for piano duets (with easy second part), which I had just composed, dedicating them respectively as follows: the March to Alfredo Casella; the Valse to Erik Satie; and the Polka to Diaghileff. I got him to play the second part of these pieces, and when we reached the Polka I told him that in composing it I had thought of him as a circus ringmaster in evening dress and top hat, cracking his whip and urging on a rider. He was discountenanced, not quite knowing whether he ought to be offended, but we had a good laugh over it together in the end.

Diaghileff was just then the center of an extensive circle in Rome. Among the new acquaintances I made I may mention Gerald Tyrwhitt, who later became Lord Berners. A great lover of art and a cultured musician, he became in succession a composer and a painter. Diaghileff later commissioned him to write the music of the ballet *The Triumph of Neptune*, which was a great success. I very much enjoyed his company, his English humor, his kindness, and his charming hospitality. I also saw Prokofiev, whom Diaghileff had summoned from Russia to discuss the composition of a ballet he had commissioned. I had already met Prokofiev in Russia, but during this stay I had an opportunity to enter into closer relationship with this remarkable musician, whose worth is now universally recognized.

Having spent a fortnight in Italy discussing various projects with Diaghileff, I climbed back again to the snows of my Chateau d'Oex. My family and I were quartered in a hotel, in which it was impossible for me to compose. I was anxious, therefore, to find a piano in some place where I could work in peace. I have never been able to compose unless sure that no one could hear me. A music dealer of whom I made my first inquiries provided me with a sort of lumber room, full of empty Chocolat Suchard packing cases, which opened on to a chicken run. It contained a little upright piano, quite new and out of tune. The cold in this room, which was devoid of any heating apparatus, was so acute that the piano strings had succumbed to it. For two days I tried to work there in overcoat, fur cap, and snowboots, with a rug over my knees. But I could not go on like that. Finally I found in the village a spacious and comfortable room in a house belonging to lower middle class folk who were out all day. I had a piano installed there, and at last could devote myself to my work. I was busy at the time with two compositions: *Les Noces* and the first sketches of a piece which became the *Renard* suite. The Russian folklore continued to entice me, and its inspirational ideas were far from exhausted. *Renard*, like *Les Noces* and the vocal pieces already mentioned, had its origin in these folk poems, and many pages of this music were composed on the original texts. The work made good progress, and I returned to Clarens well satisfied with having brought *Les Noces* to the point which I had wanted to reach before the spring.

Once there, I had at once to set about finding some place in which I could definitely settle myself with my family. I searched the neighborhood of Lausanne, and my choice fell upon Morges, a little town on the banks of the Lake of Geneva, and there I passed five years of my life.

About the same time – that is, in the spring of 1915 – Diaghileff came to see me in Switzerland, and, to my delight, established himself near me and stayed until the winter. He took Bellerive, a property at Ouchy, and I hoped and expected that we should often see one another. Unfortunately, however, my younger daughter fell ill with measles soon after his arrival, and this prevented me from visiting him for several weeks, because, as I have already explained, his fear of contagion was notorious. At Ouchy, he was surrounded by a little group, including the dancer Massine, the painters Larionov, Mme Goncharova, and Bakst, who often came over from Geneva; the famous old dancing master Cecchetti, who was working with Massine; Ansermet, whom Diaghileff had selected as conductor of the orchestra, and a little troupe of artists he had managed to collect. Everybody was getting ready for the approaching season in the United States, for which Diaghileff was then negotiating.

When all danger of contagion had at length vanished, Diaghileff, though not without misgiving, at last opened his door to me. Then, to recompense him for the long delay, I played him the first two tableaux of *Les Noces*. He was so moved, and his enthusiasm seemed so genuine and touching, that I could not but dedicate the work to him.

Diaghileff had decided that before starting for America he would give a grand gala performance in the Paris Opera House for the benefit of the Red Cross. Among other ballets, the program was to include my *Oiseau de Feu* and Massine's first choreographic creation, *Le Soleil de Minuit*, founded on selections from Rimsky-Korsakov's opera, *Snegourotchka*. Diaghileff had also been asked to give a performance for the Red Cross at Geneva, and he decided to make the occasion a sort of dress rehearsal of his new ballet, before going to Paris. He organized a festival of music and dance at the Geneva Theatre, and Félia Litvinne lent her aid and opened the matinee by singing the Russian National Anthem. I was to conduct, for first time in public, selections from *L'Oiseau de Feu* in the form of a symphonic suite, and the program included *Carnaval* and *Soleil de Minuit* conducted by Ernest Ansermet. The ballets were given in costume, but against a black backcloth, the scenery being then in Paris. It was Ansermet's debut, too, as conductor of the Russian Ballet.

The grand gala in Paris took place soon afterwards, and I went from Geneva with Diaghileff and the whole company. Paris was gloomy in those sinister days of my first visit since the declaration of war. But, in spite of that, the Red Cross grand gala was a triumphant success. It netted four hundred thousand gold francs, making a record. My debut before the Paris public as conductor of my *Oiseau* made the event of importance to me.

Diaghileff was busy preparing for the trip to America with his company. As the Metropolitan Opera House, which had made the contract with him for the New York season, wanted to see me conduct my works, he begged me to go with him, but I would not risk sailing in the absence of any definite engagement by the Metropolitan. It was Diaghileff's first trip to America, and, having an inordinate fear of the sea, he was deeply moved in taking leave of me. I myself was perturbed about him, because of the war and the submarine danger.

Before returning to Morges, I stayed a few days more in Paris to see some of my friends, notably Princess Edmond de Polignac, who always showed me much kindness. She took advantage of my presence in Paris to discuss, among other things, a little piece for drawing-room presentation which she proposed to put on at her house as soon as the war was over. I suggested *Renard* to her, which, as I have already said, I had sketched out at Chateau d'Oex. She was much pleased with the idea, and I set to work on it as soon as I got back to Morges.

I had a visit shortly afterwards from Nijinsky and his wife, whom I had not met before. They had just been released from their internment in Hungary, where the war had caught them, and were in Switzerland on their way to join the Russian Ballet in New York. Diaghileff had been working a long time for their liberation, and it had at last been achieved, in spite of innumerable difficulties which had been overcome only by the energy and extraordinary persistence of my late friend.

Greatly upset at having no news from America, the war having landed me in a situation of grave pecuniary difficulties, I asked Nijinsky, on reaching New York, to insist on my engagement being definitely settled. I was at that time in great need, and in my ingenuousness even begged Nijinsky to make his own participation in the performances depend upon my engagement. Needless to say, whatever course was taken, nothing came of it. As for Diaghileff, I learned later that he was much distressed at being unable to get the Metropolitan to engage me, as he had confidently counted upon it, and it was no less important to him than to me.

So I stayed quietly at Morges, working at *Renard*, for which I had temporarily set aside *Les Noces*. There was at that time in Geneva a little restaurant with a small orchestra of string instruments, including a cymbalon, on which Aladar Racz excelled. He is a Hungarian, and has since become recognized as a virtuoso. I was captivated by the instrument which delighted me by its rich, full tone and by the player's direct contact with the strings through the little sticks held between his fingers, and even by its trapezoid shape. I wanted to get one, and begged Racz to help me by making my wish known among his associates in Geneva, and, in fact, he did tell me of an old Hungarian who sold me one of these instruments. I carried it off to Morges in glee, and very soon learned to play it well enough to enable me to compose a part for cymbalon which I introduced into the little orchestra of *Renard*.

I saw a great deal of Ramuz at this time, as we were working together at the French translation of the Russian text of my *Pribaoutki*, *Berceuses du Chat* and *Renard*. I initiated him into the peculiarities and subtle shades of the Russian language, and the difficulties presented by its tonic accent. I was astonished at his insight, his intuitive ability, and his gift for transferring the spirit and poesy of the Russian folk poems to a language so remote and different as French.

I was very much wrapped up in this collaboration which

cemented still more firmly the bonds of our friendship and affinity of mind.

I awaited Diaghileff's return from America with impatience and excitement. He sent me word in March of his arrival in Spain, and I at once took the train to join him. He told me of the terrible fears which he had experienced in crossing by an Italian ship, laden with munitions of war, which had constantly had to change its course by reason of warnings of submarines. They even had a rehearsal of an alarm, and I still possess a photograph which Diaghileff gave me in which he is wearing his lifesaving apparatus.

It was my first visit to Spain, and I was struck by much that I saw directly I crossed the frontier. First there was the change in railway gauge, exactly as in Russia. I expected to find different weights and measures; but, not at all! Although the railways were different, the metric system prevailed as in the greater part of the globe. At the very boundary the smell of frying in oil became perceptible. When I reached Madrid at nine o'clock in the morning I found the whole town still fast asleep, and I was received at my hotel by the night watchman with lantern in hand. Yet it was spring. The people rose late, and life was in full swing after midnight. At a fixed hour every day I heard from my room the distant sound of a *banda* playing a *passadoble*, and military exercises always apparently ended with that sort of music. All the little characteristics of the Spaniards' daily life pleased me immensely, and I experienced and savored them with great gusto. They struck me as marking a vivid change from the monotony of the impressions generally received in passing from one European country to another, for the countries of Europe differ far less among themselves than all of them together do from this land on the edge of our continent, where already one is in touch with Africa.

"I have been waiting for you like a brother," were Diaghileff's first words. And, indeed, I felt all the pleasure he was experiencing in seeing me again, for I was a friend upon whose feelings he could rely and with whom he could let himself go after his long loneliness. Diaghileff and the new acquaintances I made in Madrid made my stay there very agreeable. I treasure my recollections of it all the more because it was then that I met Mme Eugenia de Errazuris, a Chilean lady who had preserved almost intact marks of great beauty and perfect distinction. The sympathy she showed at our first encounter, and which later developed into unfailing friendship, touched me deeply, and I enjoyed her subtle and unrivaled understanding of an art which was not that of her generation.

While I was in Madrid, Diaghileff was producing his ballets at the Royal Theatre, where *L'Oiseau de Feu* and *Petroushka* were among those given, and where I had the honor of being presented to the King and the two Queens.

I must record the tremendous impression made on me by Toledo and the Escorial. My two short excursions to them showed me a Spain for which I should have searched in vain in historic treatises. My glimpses of these two places evoked in me visions not so much of the horrors of the Inquisition or the cruelties of the days of tyranny as a revelation of the profoundly religious temperament of the people and the mystic fervor of their Catholicism, so closely akin in its essentials to the religious feeling and spirit of Russia. I especially noticed the difference which exists between the Catholicism of Spain and that of Rome, which impresses all observers by the impassive grandeur of its authority. I found a logical explanation of that difference in the consideration that the Catholicism of Rome, as the Metropolis and center of Western Christianity, must necessarily wear a more austere and

63

immutable aspect than the Catholicism of the outlying countries.

Do not be astonished if I say nothing about Spanish folk music. I do not dispute its distinctive character, but for me there was no revelation in it. That, however, did not prevent me from frequenting taverns to spend whole evenings in listening to the endless preliminary chords of guitar playing and to a deep-voiced singer with unending breath trolling forth her long Arab ballad with a wealth of *fioriture*.

Throughout the whole summer and autumn I was busied in finishing the music of *Renard* and in adapting Ramuz's French translation to the notation. At the same time I wrote some little pieces for piano duets, with an easy right hand, for amateurs little practiced in the use of the instrument, the whole burden of the composition being concentrated in the left-hand part. I enjoyed solving this little problem, which served as a pendant to the *Trois Pièces Faciles* (March, Polka, and Valse) already mentioned, in which I had done exactly the opposite, making the left hand easy. These little compositions I called *Cinq Pièces Faciles* (Andante, Napolitana, Espagnola, Balalaïka, Galop). I subsequently orchestrated them and the three earlier ones, and, after some years' interval, they appeared in the form of two suites, each containing four pieces, for a small orchestra, and they are often found in symphony concert programs. They are sometimes played separately, but I prefer to conduct the two in sequence, as they are designed to complement one another. In the same period I composed also the four choruses for women's voices *a capella* of which I spoke in connection with Russian folk poetry, and likewise three little songs for children: *Tilim-Bum*, which I orchestrated and slightly amplified at a later date; *Chanson de l'Ours*, and a *Berceuse* for

64

my little daughter, with my own words. All these vocal pieces have been translated into French by Ramuz, but the last two have not been published.

Some of my friends at that time offered to bear the cost of publishing several of my compositions. I gave the work to Henn, the Geneva concert agent, and *Renard, Pribaoutki, Berceuses du Chat*, and the two groups of easy pieces for duets thus made their appearance in the winter of 1916-1917. The attention which I had to give to the publication of this music, the selection of paper, style of printing, pagination, cover, and so forth, took no little time, but also gave me no little enjoyment.

Just before Christmas I had to interrupt everything I was doing. I suffered excruciating pain from a severe attack of intercostal neuralgia, and there were moments when I could scarcely breathe. Dr. Demieville, a professor at Lausanne, pulled me through, and at the New Year I began to live again, but the convalescence was a long one. My legs were almost paralyzed as the result of my illness, and I could not move without assistance. I shudder even now at the thought of what I had to endure.

Before I had fully recovered, Diaghileff, having heard that I was ill, came to see me. In the course of our talks, he proposed that he should put on *Le Rossignol* in ballet form, as he had already done with *Le Coq d'Or*. I rejoined with a counter-proposition. I had been thinking of making a symphonic poem for the orchestra by combining the music of the second and third acts of *Le Rossignol*, which were homogeneous, and I told Diaghileff that I would place that at his disposal if he cared to make a ballet of it. He warmly welcomed the suggestion, and I adapted a scenario from Andersen's fairy story to serve the purpose. I at once set myself to the arrangement of this poem, without altogether setting aside *Les Noces*, which I had taken up again with the expectation of finishing it very soon.

Diaghileff had gone to Rome, where he was to have a Russian Ballet season, and begged me to join him to conduct *L'Oiseau de Feu* and *Feu d'Artifice*, for the latter of which he had commissioned the Italian futurist, Balla, to prepare a special *décor* with lighting effects. When I reached Rome in March I found in the apartment Diaghileff had rented quite a large assembly gathered round his lavishly hospitable table. There were Ansermet, Bakst, Picasso, whom I then met for the first time, Cocteau, Balla, Lord Berners, Massine, and many others. The season at the Costanzi Theatre opened with a gala performance for the Italian Red Cross, at which I conducted *L'Oiseau de Feu* and *Feu d'Artifice* with the Balla setting.

The February Revolution had just taken place in Russia, the Tsar had abdicated, and a Provisional Government was in power. In normal times a Russian gala performance would have begun with the National Anthem, but at that date nothing could have been more inept than to sing *God Save the Tsar*. It was necessary to find some substitute for it, and the idea of opening the performance with a Russian folk song suggested itself to Diaghileff, who chose the famous *Volga Boat Song*. But the orchestra would have to play it, and there was no instrumentation; it had not been scored. Diaghileff besought me to get on with it as quickly as possible, so I had to sacrifice myself, and throughout the whole night preceding the gala I sat at the piano in Lord Berners' apartment instrumenting and scoring the song for the orchestra, dictating it chord by chord, note by note, to Ansermet, who wrote it down. The orchestra parts were then quickly copied out, and in that way I was able to hear my own instrumentation, conducted by Ansermet, at the next morning's rehearsal of the evening program. The performance in the evening began with the Italian National Anthem, followed by the *Boat Song*, in place of Russia's. I conducted *L'Oiseau de Feu* and *Feu d'Artifice* with its *décor*, with special lighting effects.

I can still recall the big reception that Diaghileff gave in the Grand Hotel in the course of my stay, at which I conducted parts of *Petroushka*, and at which there was an exhibition of cubist and futurist pictures by his friends and collaborators.

Diaghileff, Picasso, Massine, and I went on from Rome to Naples. Ansermet had gone in advance to prepare for the performances that Diaghileff was to give there.

Instead of the sunshine and azure blue I had expected at Naples, I found a leaden sky, the summit of Vesuvius being shrouded in immovable and ominous mist. Still, I retain happy memories of my fortnight in this town, half Spanish and half reminiscent of the Near East. The company stayed on to rehearse Massine's second ballet, *The Good-humored Ladies*, in an appropriate setting with Scarlatti's music, as orchestrated by Tommasini. Bakst, the designer of the *décor* and costumes, had come for the rehearsals. Massine, who from the beginning had shown himself to be a ballet master of great talent, had created an admirable choreographic representation of Goldoni's charming story. I took advantage of my leisure to inspect the town, generally in Picasso's company. The famous aquarium attracted us more than anything else, and we spent hours there. We had both been greatly taken by the old Neapolitan water colors and fairly combed all the little shops and dealers' establishments in the course of our frequent expeditions.

From Naples I went back to Rome, where I had a delightful week with Lord Berners. I shall never forget the adventure which later befell me in crossing the frontier at Chiasso on my return to Switzerland. I was taking my portrait, which Picasso had just drawn at Rome and given to me. When the military authorities examined my luggage they found this drawing, and nothing in the world would induce them to let it pass. They asked me what it represented, and when I told them that it was my portrait, drawn by a distinguished artist, they utterly refused to believe me. "It is not a portrait, but a plan," they said. "Yes, the plan of my face, but of nothing else," I replied. But all my efforts failed to convince them, and I had to send the portrait, in Lord Berners' name, to the British Ambassador in Rome, who later forwarded it to Paris in the diplomatic bag. The altercation made me miss my connection, and I had to stay at Chiasso till next day.

Alas! a cruel and unexpected blow was to overwhelm me with sorrow just after I reached home. An old friend of ours, who had entered my parents' service before I was born and had looked after me in my earliest days, a friend to whom I was closely attached and whom I loved as a second mother, was then living with us at Morges, as I had made her come to us at the beginning of the war. Not long after my return, I lunched with Ramuz at his house in Lausanne and on returning home in his company I noticed a stranger in tail coat and top hat in my garden. Surprised, I asked him what he wanted. "It appears that there has been a death in the house," he said. That was how I learned of the loss that had befallen me. In the space of a few short hours the bursting of a blood vessel had carried off my old Bertha. There had not even been time to warn me at Lausanne.

Several weeks went by in sorrow before I could resume

my work. Change of scene put me on my feet again – we went into the mountains for the summer, to Diablerets. But I had scarcely got back to work when I had the shock of a new grief. A telegram from Russia informed me that my brother, in the army on the Roumanian front, had just succumbed to typhus. I had not seen him for a long time, as he had been living in Russia and I abroad, but, though our lives had been very diverse, I had remained deeply attached to him, and the news of his death brought me acute grief.

During this difficult time I was fortunately able to find some distraction in the frequent visits of such friends as Ramuz, Berners, Diaghileff, and Ansermet. I continued working at the last scene of *Les Noces* during the summer, and I finished a piece for the pianola. Many of the musicians who had preceded me in visiting Spain had, on their return, put their impressions on record in works devoted to the music they had heard there, Glinka having far outshone the rest with his incomparable *La Jota Aragonaise* and *Une Nuit à Madrid*. It was probably in order to conform to this custom that I, too, paid tribute to it. The whimsicalities of the un-expected melodies of the mechanical pianos and rattletrap orchestrinas of the Madrid streets and the little night taverns served as theme for this piece, which I wrote expressly for the pianola, and which was published as a roll by the London Aeolian Company. Subsequently, I orchestrated this piece, which was called *Madrid*, and formed part of my *Quatre Etudes pour Orchestre*, the others being the three pieces originally written as quartets in 1914.

V

This period, the end of 1917, was one of the hardest I have ever experienced. Overwhelmed by the successive bereavements that I had suffered, I was now also in a position of the utmost pecuniary difficulty. The Communist Revolution, which had just triumphed in Russia, deprived me of the last resources which had still from time to time been reaching me from my country, and I found myself, so to speak, face to face with nothing, in a foreign land and right in the middle of the war.

It was imperative to find some way of ensuring a tolerable existence for my family. My only consolation was to see that I was not alone in suffering from these circumstances. My friends Ramuz, Ansermet, and many others were all in equally straitened circumstances. We often met and sought feverishly for some means of escape from this alarming situation. It was in these talks that Ramuz and I got hold of the idea of creating a sort of little traveling theatre, easy to transport from place to place and to show in even small localities. But for that we had to have funds, and these were absolutely lacking. We discussed this mad enterprise with Ansermet, who was to become its orchestra leader, and with Auberjonois, whose province was to be the *décor* and costumes. We elaborated our project to the last detail, even to the itinerary of the tour, and all this on empty pockets. We had to find a wealthy patron or a group who could be persuaded to interest themselves in our scheme. It was, alas! no easy matter. Refusals not always polite, but always categoric, greeted us every time. At last, however, we had the good fortune to meet someone who not only promised to collect the requisite capital, but entered into our plan with cordiality and sympathetic encouragement. It was M. Werner Reinhart of Winterthur, famous for his broad intellectual culture and the generous support that he and his brothers extended to the arts and to artists.

Under this patronage, we set ourselves to work. Afanasyev's famous collection of Russian tales, in which I was then deeply absorbed, provided me with the subject of our performance. I introduced them to Ramuz, who was very responsive to Russian folklore, and immediately shared my enthusiasm. For the purpose of our theatre we were particularly drawn to the cycle of legends dealing with the adventures of the soldier who deserted and the Devil who inexorably comes to carry off his soul. This cycle was based on folk stories of a cruel period of enforced recruitment under Nicholas I, a period which also produced many songs known as *Rekroutskia*, which expatiate in verse on the tears and lamentations of women robbed of their sons or sweethearts.

Although the character of their subject is specifically Russian, these songs depict situations and sentiments and unfold a moral so common to the human race as to make an international appeal. It was this essentially human aspect of the tragic story of the soldier destined to become the prey of the Devil that attracted Ramuz and myself.

So we worked at our task with great zest, reminding ourselves frequently of the modest means at our disposal to carry it to completion. I knew only too well that so far as the music was concerned I should have to be content with a very restricted orchestra. The easiest solution would have been to use some such polyphonic instrument as the piano or harmonium. The latter was out of the question, chiefly because of its dynamic poverty, due to the complete absence of accents.

Though the piano has polyphonic qualities infinitely more varied, and offers many particularly dynamic possibilities, I had to avoid it for two reasons: either my score would have seemed like an arrangement for the piano, and that would have given evidence of a certain lack of financial means, which would not have been at all in keeping with our intentions, or I should have had to use it as a solo instrument, exploiting every possibility of its technique. In other words, I should have had to be specially careful about the "pianism" of my score, and make it into a vehicle of virtuosity, in order to justify my choice of medium. So there was nothing for it but to decide on a group of instruments, a selection which would include the most representative types, in treble and bass, of the instrumental families: for the strings, the violin and the double bass; for the wood, the clarinet, because it has the biggest compass, and the bassoon; for the brass, trumpet and trombone, and, finally, the percussion manipulated by only one musician, the whole, of course, under a conductor. Another consideration which made this idea particularly attractive to me was the interest afforded to the spectator by being able to see these instrumentalists each playing his own part in the ensemble. I have always had a horror of listening to music with my eyes shut, with nothing for them to do. The sight of the gestures and movements of the various parts of the body producing the music is fundamentally necessary if it is to be grasped in all its fullness. All music created or composed demands some exteriorization for the perception of the listener. In other words, it must have an intermediary, an executant. That being an essential condition, without which music cannot wholly reach us, why wish to ignore it, or try to do so – why shut the eyes to this fact which is inherent in the very nature of musical art?

Obviously one frequently prefers to turn away one's eyes, or even close them, when the superfluity of the player's gesticulations prevents the concentration of one's faculties of hearing. But if the player's movements are evoked solely by the exigencies of the music, and do not tend to make an impression on the listener by extramusical devices, why not follow with the eye such movements as those of the drummer, the violinist, or the trombonist, which facilitate one's auditory perceptions? As a matter of fact, those who maintain that they only enjoy music to the full with their eyes shut do not hear better than when they have them open, but the absence of visual distractions enables them to abandon themselves to the reveries induced by the lullaby of its sounds, and that is really what they prefer to the music itself.

These ideas induced me to have my little orchestra well in evidence when planning *L'Histoire d'un Soldat*. It was to be on one side of the stage, and a small dais for the reader on the other. This arrangement established the connection between the three elements of the piece which by their close cooperation were to form a unity: in the center, the stage and the actors; on one side of them the music, and, on the other, the reader. Our idea was that the three elements should sometimes take turns as soloists and sometimes combine as an ensemble.

We worked hard at *L'Histoire d'un Soldat* during all the early part of 1918, as we intended to produce it in the summer. My uninterrupted collaboration with Ramuz was the more precious to me because our friendship, growing closer and closer, helped me to bear the difficult times through which I was living, sickened and, as a patriot, desperately humiliated, as I was by the monstrous Peace of Brest-Litovsk. When we had finished writing the *Soldat*, a

73

lively and amusing time ensued. We had to arrange for its staging, and for that we had first of all to find actors. By good luck it happened that George and Ludmila Pitoëff were at Geneva just then, and lent us their valuable assistance; he as the Devil in his dancing scenes, and she as the Princess. Two more actors were needed – for the role of the Soldier and of the Devil where he was only acting. We required also a reader, and we found all three among the Lausanne University students. Gabriel Rossel took the part of the Soldier, Jean Villard that of the Devil, and the young geologist, Elie Gagnebin, became the reader.

After a great many rehearsals for the actors, for the musicians, and for the Princess' dances, which Mme Pitoëff and I evolved together, we reached the moment to which we had so eagerly looked forward, and on September 28, 1918, the first performance was given – at the Lausanne Theatre.

I had always been a sincere admirer of René Auberjonois' drawing and painting, but I had not expected that he would give proof of such subtle imagination and such complete mastery as he did in the scenery and costumes and the whole artistry of his setting. Among our other collaborators I had had the good fortune to discover one who later became not only a most faithful and devoted friend, but also one of the most reliable and understanding executants of my compositions: I mean Ansermet.

I had already recommended him to Diaghileff to take the place of Pierre Monteux, who, greatly to our regret, had had to leave us to take up the direction of the Boston Symphony Orchestra, and I valued very highly his admirable gifts of musicianship, the firmness of his conducting, and his broad general culture, but up to that time I had not been able to form a definite opinion of him as conductor of my own works.

He was frequently absent, and it was, therefore, only rarely and by chance that I had had any opportunity of hearing him conduct my music; and the few isolated renderings I had heard, good though they were, had not been sufficient to show me what an admirable conductor he was to become, and how faithfully he could transmit my musical thought to the public, without ever falsifying it by personal or arbitrary interpretation. For, as I have already said, music should be transmitted and not interpreted, because interpretation reveals the personality of the interpreter rather than that of the author, and who can guarantee that such an executant will reflect the author's vision without distortion?

An executant's talent lies precisely in his faculty for seeing what is actually in the score, and certainly not in a determination to find there what he would like to find. This is Ansermet's greatest and most precious quality, and it particularly revealed itself while we were studying the score of the *Soldat*. From that moment dates an intellectual understanding between us which time has only increased and strengthened.

His reputation as a perfect executant of my works is well established, but I have always been astonished that many apparently cultured people who admire his execution of contemporary music, do not pay enough attention to the way in which he renders the works of days gone by. Ansermet is one of the conductors who emphatically confirm my long-standing conviction that it is impossible for anyone to grasp fully the art of a bygone period, to penetrate beneath the obsolete form and discern the author's meaning in a language no longer spoken, unless he has a comprehensive and lively feeling for the present, and unless he consciously participates in the life around him.

For it is only those who are essentially alive who can

75

discover the real life of those who are "dead." That is why, even from a pedagogical point of view, I think that it would be wiser to begin the education of a pupil by first giving him a knowledge of what is, and only then tracing history backward, step by step, to what has been.

Frankly, I have but little confidence in those who pose as refined connoisseurs and passionate admirers of the great pontiffs of art – honored by several stars in the guidebooks or by a portrait, usually quite unrecognizable, in illustrated encyclopedias – but who know nothing of the art of their own times. Should any consideration at all be given to those who go into raptures over great names but whose attitude, when confronted with contemporary works, is one of bored indifference, or the display of a marked preference for the mediocre and the commonplace?

Ansermet's merit lies precisely in his ability to reveal the relationship between the music of today and that of the past by purely musical methods. Knowing, as he does to perfection, the musical language of our own times, and, on the other hand, playing a large number of old, classical scores, he soon perceived that the authors of all periods were confronted by the solution of problems which were, above all, specifically musical. That is his rare merit, and that explains his vital contact with the musical literature of the most diverse periods.

With regard to technique in the true sense of the word, to give a rendering of the *Soldat* was a brilliant opportunity for Ansermet to display his mastery. For with an orchestra of only seven musicians, all playing as soloists, there could be no question of fooling the public by the dynamic effects with which we were all familiar and which are all too easy; it was necessary not only to reach a meticulous perfection and precision of execution, but to sustain it without ever faltering for a moment, because, with so small a number of instruments, it would have been impossible to conceal what an adroit conductor could have made to pass unnoticed in a large orchestra.

Taking all these things into consideration, the first performance of the *Soldat* completely satisfied me. Nor was this so from the point of view of music only. It was a great success as a whole, thanks to careful execution, setting, and perfect interpretation. The true note was struck then, but unfortunately I have never since seen a performance of the *Soldat* that has satisfied me to the same degree. I have kept a special place in my memory for that performance, and I am grateful to my friends and collaborators, as well as to Werner Reinhart, who, having been unable to find any other backers, generously financed the whole enterprise himself. As a token of my gratitude and friendship, I wrote for, and dedicated to, him three pieces for clarinet solo, he being familiar with that instrument and liking to play it among his intimates.

As I have already indicated, we had no intention of restricting the *Soldat* to one performance. We had much more extensive plans, and meant to go further afield in Switzerland with our traveling theatre. But, alas! we had reckoned without the Spanish influenza which was raging all over Europe at that time and did not spare us. One after another we all fell victims to it; we, our families, and even the agents who were to have taken charge of our tour. All our beautiful dreams faded away.

Before talking of my return to life after this long and depressing illness, I must go back a little to mention a work which I composed directly after finishing the score of the *Soldat*. Its dimensions are modest, but it is indicative of the passion I felt at that time for jazz, which burst into life so suddenly when the war ended. At my request, a whole pile of this music was sent to me, enchanting me by its truly popular appeal, its freshness, and the novel rhythm which so distinctly revealed its Negro origin. These impressions suggested the idea of creating a composite portrait of this new dance music, giving the creation the importance of a concert piece, as, in the past, the composers of their periods had done for the minuet, the waltz, the mazurka, etc. So I composed my *Ragtime* for eleven instruments, wind, string, percussion, and a Hungarian cymbalon. Some years later, I conducted it myself at its first audition at one of Koussevitsky's concerts at the Paris Opera House.

I felt so weak after my long bout with influenza that I found it impossible at the moment to undertake anything at all fatiguing, and I therefore occupied myself with work that I imagined would not overtax my strength. I had long toyed with the idea of arranging certain fragments of *L'Oiseau de Feu* in the form of a suite, but for a much smaller orchestra, in order to facilitate its production by the many orchestral societies which, though wishing to include that work in their programs, were frequently deterred by difficulties of a purely material nature. In the earlier suite, which I had arranged shortly after the composition of the ballet, I had retained an orchestra of the same size as the original, and the various societies which organized concerts rarely had such large ensembles at their disposal. In this second version I added certain portions and cut out others which had been in the first, and I considerably decreased the orchestra without upsetting the equilibrium of the instrumental groups, so as to reduce the number needed for its performance to about sixty musicians.

As the work progressed, I saw that my task was by no means so simple as I had imagined, and it took six months to complete it.

During the winter I made the acquaintance of a Croat singer, Mme Maja de Strozzi-Pecic, who had a beautiful soprano voice. She asked me to write something for her, and I composed *Four Russian Songs* on folk poems that Ramuz translated for me.

I went to Paris in the early spring on a short visit, and there I met Diaghileff, whom I had not seen for more than a year.

The Peace of Brest-Litovsk had placed him, as it did so many of his compatriots, in a very awkward position. It had found him and his company in Spain, and there they were, so to speak, shut up, because everywhere Russians were, one and all, regarded as undesirable, and innumerable difficulties were made whenever they wished to travel from one country to another.

Having made an engagement with the London Coliseum, Diaghileff, after a great deal of trouble, did finally manage to get permission for himself and the whole company to go to London via France.

When I saw him in Paris, I naturally told him about the *Soldat*, and the pleasure that its success had given me, but he did not evince the least interest. I knew him too well to be surprised: he was incredibly jealous about his friends and collaborators, especially those he most esteemed. He simply would not recognize their right to work apart from him and his undertakings. He could not help it; he regarded their action as a breach of faith. He even found it difficult to tolerate my appearance at concerts, whether as conductor or pianist, though that obviously had nothing whatever to do with the theatre. Now that he is dead, it all seems rather touching, and it has left no trace of bitterness; but when I tried during his lifetime to get him to share in my enjoyment of successes which I had made without his participation, and encountered only his obvious indifference, or even hostility, it hurt me; I was repelled, and I suffered acutely. It was as though a friend's door had remained tightly shut after I had knocked at it. All this happened when the question of the *Soldat* arose, and a certain coolness between us ensued, but it did not last long.

While I was in Paris, Diaghileff used all his diplomatic talents to entice me – the lost sheep, so to speak – back into the fold of the Russian Ballet. In order to distract me from the unfortunate *Soldat*, he talked with exaggerated enthusiasm about his plan to put on *Le Chant du Rossignol*, with scenery and costumes by Henri Matisse and choreography by Massine. But I was not taken with the idea, because, despite the fact that the thought of collaborating with a great artist like Matisse and such a choreographer as Massine was very alluring, I had destined *Le Chant du Rossignol* for the concert platform, and a choreographic rendering seemed to me to be quite unnecessary. Its subtle and meticulous writing and its somewhat static character would not have lent themselves to stage action and the movements of dancing. But another proposal by Diaghileff did very greatly tempt me.

The success of *The Good-humored Ladies*, with Domenico Scarlatti's music, had suggested the idea of producing something to the music of another illustrious Italian, Pergolesi, whom, as he knew, I liked and admired immensely. In his visits to Italy, Diaghileff had gone through a number of this master's unfinished manuscripts that he discovered in various Italian conservatoires, copies of which he had had made for him. He later completed the collection with what he found in the libraries of London. There was a very considerable amount of material, which Diaghileff showed to me, urging that I should seek my inspiration in it and compose the music for a ballet, the subject of which was to be taken from a collection containing various versions of the amorous adventures of Pulcinella.

I have always been enchanted by Pergolesi's Neapolitan music, so entirely of the people and yet so exotic in its Spanish character. The proposal that I should work with Picasso, who was to do the scenery and costumes and whose art was particularly near and dear to me, recollections of our walks together and the impressions of Naples we had shared, the great pleasure I had experienced from Massine's choreography in *The Good-humored Ladies* – all this combined to overcome my reluctance. For it was a delicate task to breathe new life into scattered fragments and to create a whole from the isolated pages of a musician for whom I felt a special liking and tenderness.

Before attempting a task so arduous, I had to find an answer to a question of the greatest importance by which I found myself faced. Should my line of action with regard to Pergolesi be dominated by my love or by my respect for his music? Is it love or respect that urges us to possess a woman? Is it not by love alone that we succeed in penetrating to the very essence of a being? But, then, does love diminish respect? Respect alone remains barren, and can never serve as a productive or creative factor. In order to create there must be a dynamic force, and what force is more potent than love? To me it seems that to ask the question is to answer it.

I do not want the reader to think that in writing this I am trying to exonerate myself from the absurd accusations of sacrilege leveled against me. I am only too familiar with the mentality of those curators and archivists of music who jealously guard the intangibility of relics at which they never so much as look, while resenting any attempt on the part of others to resuscitate these treasures which they themselves regard as dead and sacrosanct. Not only is my conscience clear of having committed sacrilege, but, so far as I can see, my attitude towards Pergolesi is the only one that can usefully be taken up with regard to the music of bygone times.

Instead of starting work on the *Pulcinella* directly, I returned to Morges, and finished a piano piece I had begun some time before with Artur Rubinstein and his strong, agile, clever fingers in mind. I dedicated this *Piano Rag Music* to him. I was inspired by the same ideas, and my aim was the same, as in *Ragtime*, but in this case I stressed the percussion possibilities of the piano. What fascinated me most of all in the work was that the different rhythmic episodes were dictated by the fingers themselves. My own fingers seemed to enjoy it so much that I began to practice the piece; not that I wanted to play it in public – my pianistic repertoire even today is too limited to fill a recital program – but simply for my personal satisfaction. Fingers are not to be despised: they are great inspirers, and, in contact with a musical instrument, often give birth to subconscious ideas which might otherwise never come to life. During the following months I gave myself up entirely to *Pulcinella*, and the work filled me with joy. The material I had at my disposal – numerous fragments and shreds of compositions either unfinished or merely outlined, which by good fortune had eluded filtering academic editors – made me appreciate more and more the true nature of Pergolesi while discerning ever more clearly the closeness of my mental and, so to speak, sensory kinship with him.

Frequent conferences with Diaghileff, Picasso, and Massine were necessitated by the task before me – which was to write a ballet for a definite scenario, with scenes differing in character but following each other in ordered sequence. I therefore had to go to Paris from time to time in order to settle every detail. Our conferences were very often far from peaceable; frequent disagreements arose, and our meetings occasionally ended in stormy scenes.

Sometimes the costumes failed to come up to Diaghileff's expectations; sometimes my orchestration disappointed him. Massine composed his choreography from a piano arrangement made from the orchestral score and sent piecemeal to him by me as I finished each part. As a result of this, it often happened that when I was shown certain steps and movements that had been decided upon I saw to my horror that in character and importance they in nowise corresponded to the very modest possibilities of my small chamber orchestra. They had wanted, and looked for, something quite different from my score, something it could not give. The choreography had, therefore, to be altered and adapted to the volume of my music, and that caused them no little annoyance, though they realized that there was no other solution.

In the autumn, Werner Reinhart was good enough to organize some concerts in Geneva, Lausanne, and Zürich to let the Swiss public hear something of my chamber music, such as the suite *L'Histoire d'un Soldat* for piano, violin, and clarinet; the three solo pieces for clarinet only; the two small groups of songs *Berceuses du Chat* and *Pribaoutki*; *Ragtime*, arranged as a piano solo; *Piano Rag Music*; and

83

finally, the eight easy duets for the piano. My executants were Mlle. Tatianova, vocalist; José Iturbi, pianist; José Porta, violinist; and Edmond Allegra, clarinet. Iturbi and I played the duets.

I ought to mention here a concert which had a certain importance for me in view of my new orchestral experiments. On December 6 a first performance of *Le Chant du Rossignol* was given at Geneva at one of the subscription concerts of the Orchestre de la Suisse Romande under the direction of Ernest Ansermet. I say new experiment because, in this symphonic poem, written for an orchestra of ordinary size, I treated the latter more as a chamber orchestra, and laid stress on the *concertante* side, not only of the various solo instruments, but also gave this role to whole groups of instruments. This orchestral treatment was well adapted to music full of cadenzas, vocalises, and melismata of all kinds, and in which *tutti* were the exception. I enjoyed the performance greatly, for the rendering was careful and highly finished. I reached the conclusion – very regretfully, since I was the author of many works for the threatre – that a perfect rendering can be achieved only in the concert hall, because the stage presents a combination of several elements upon which the music has often to depend, so that it cannot rely upon the exclusive consideration which it receives at a concert. I was confirmed in this view when two months later, under the direction of the same conductor, Ansermet, *Le Chant du Rossignol* was given as a ballet by Diaghileff at the Paris Opera.

All the early part of 1920 was filled with excitement, feverish activity, and continual travel necessitated by preparations for the performance of *Pulcinella*, which was given at the Opera on May 15. I had to go to and fro between

Morges and Paris, where my presence was constantly required either to hear singers and rehearse them, or to follow closely the choreographic rehearsals in order to spare Massine unpleasant misunderstandings of the sort already described.

Although all this was very tiring, I enjoyed taking part in a task which ended in a real success. *Pulcinella* is one of those productions – and they are rare – where everything harmonizes, where all the elements – subject, music, dancing, and artistic setting – form a coherent and homogeneous whole. As for the choreography, with the possible exception of a few episodes that it had not been possible to change, it is one of Massine's finest creations, so fully has he assimilated the spirit of the Neapolitan theatre. In addition, his own performance in the title role was above all praise. As for Picasso, he worked miracles, and I find it difficult to decide what was most enchanting – the coloring, the design, or the amazing inventiveness of this remarkable man.

I had expected a hostile reception from those who have constituted themselves the custodians of scholastic tradition, and was not astonished by their reprobation. I had formed the habit of disregarding this equivocal musical group whose authority was more than doubtful. All the more precious was the attitude of those who were able to discern in my score something better than a more or less adroit eighteenth-century *pastiche*.

As, with the return of peace, life resumed its activities in the whole of Europe, particularly in France, I realized that I could no longer remain in the involuntary isolation to which the war had confined me. I therefore resolved to take my lares and penates to France, where, at the moment, the pulse of the world was throbbing most strongly. It was with a full heart that I felt constrained to bid adieu to the

Vaud country, which had endeared itself to me by the precious friendships found in it, and which had helped me bear the severe trials that I had had to undergo during the war years. I shall always keep in my heart a feeling of affection for it.

In June I left Morges with my family and settled in France. We spent the summer in Brittany. It was an important moment in my life, for it closed one period of it. The ensuing period takes on a wider aspect, thanks to the fact that, while still continuing my creative work, I became also the executant of my own music. I shall have occasion to speak of this new activity, and the reflections to which it gives rise, in the second part of my *chronique*, where I shall record my life from the time when I settled in France, which had become my second motherland.

TWO: Composer and Performer

VI

When I left Switzerland to settle in France I brought away some sketches of an idea suggested by M. Alfred Pochon, leader of the Flonzaley String Quartet. The Flonzaley, a group of Vaudois musicians, taking their name from that canton, performed in the United States for a considerable time. M. Pochon wished to introduce a contemporary work into their almost exclusively classical repertoire, and asked me to write them an ensemble piece, in form and length of my own choosing, to appear in the programs of their numerous tours.

So it was for them that I composed my *Concertino*, a piece in one single movement, treated in the form of a free sonata allegro with a definitely *concertante* part for first violin, and this, on account of its limited dimensions, led me to give it the diminutive title: *Concertino (piccolo concerto)*.

During my stay at Carantec, in Brittany, I was also engaged on another work, which originated as follows:

The *Revue Musicale* proposed to issue a number devoted to the memory of Debussy, containing several pages of music, each specially written for the occasion by one of the great man's surviving admirers, and I was among those asked to contribute.

The composition of this page, however, made me feel bound to give rein to the development of a new phase of musical thought conceived under the influence of the work itself and the solemnity of the circumstances that had led to it.

I began at the end, and wrote a choral piece which later on became the final section of my *Symphonies pour Instruments à Vent*, dedicated to the memory of Claude Achille Debussy. This I gave to the *Revue Musicale* in a version arranged for the pianoforte.

It was while still in Switzerland that I heard of Debussy's death. When I had last seen him he was already very weak, and I realized that he must soon leave us. Subsequently I had received more reassuring accounts of him, so that the news of his death came upon me rather unexpectedly.

I was sincerely attached to him as a man, and I grieved not only at the loss of one whose great friendship had been marked with unfailing kindness towards myself and my work, but at the passing of an artist who, in spite of maturity and health already hopelessly undermined, had still been able to retain his creative powers to the full, and whose musical genius had been in no way impaired throughout the whole period of his activity.

While composing my *Symphonies* I naturally had in mind the man to whom I wished to dedicate them. I used to wonder what impression my music would have made on him, and what his reactions would have been. I had a distinct feeling that he would have been rather disconcerted by my musical idiom, as he was, I remember, by my *Roi des Etoiles*, also dedicated to him, when we played it together as a duet for one pianoforte. Moreover, this piece had been composed at the time of the *Sacre*, about seven years before the *Symphonies*. I had certainly experienced considerable evolution since then, and not in the direction pointed to by the tendencies of the Debussyist period. But this supposition, I will even say this certainty, that my music would have remained foreign to him, was far from discouraging me.

According to my idea, the homage that I intended to pay to the memory of the great musician ought not to be inspired by his musical thought; on the contrary, I desired rather to express myself in a language which should be essentially my own.

It is in the nature of things – and it is this which determines the uninterrupted march of evolution in art quite as much as in other branches of human activity – that epochs which immediately precede us are temporarily farther away from us than others which are more remote in time. That is why I do not think at the moment of writing (1935) I could form a just appreciation of Debussy. It is clear that his aesthetic, and that of his period, could not nowadays stimulate my appetite or provide food for my musical thought, though that in nowise prevents me from recognizing his outstanding personality or from drawing a distinction between him and his numerous satellites.

I finished the *Symphonies* at Garches, where I spent the winter of 1920–1921. At the same time I wrote a group of little pieces for children which were published under the title *Les Cinq Doigts*. In these eight pieces, which are very easy, the five fingers of the right hand, once on the keys, remain in the same place sometimes even for the whole length of the piece, while the left hand, which is destined to accompany the melody, executes a pattern, either harmonic or contrapuntal, of the utmost simplicity. I found it rather amusing, with these very much restricted means, to try to awaken in the child a taste for melodic design in its combinations with a rudimentary accompaniment.

Diaghileff was just then giving a new production of *Le Sacre du Printemps* at the Théatre des Champs-Elysées.

Nijinsky's absence – he had been interned for some years – and the impossibility of remembering his overburdened, complicated, and confused choreography, gave us the idea of re-creating it in a more living form, and the work was entrusted to Léonide Massine.

The young ballet master accomplished his task with unquestionable talent.

He certainly put order and understanding into his dance compositions. There were even moments of great beauty in the group movements when the plastic expression was in perfect accord with the music, and, above all, in the sacrificial dance so brilliantly executed by Lydia Sokolova that it still lives in the memory of everyone who saw it. I must say, however, that, notwithstanding its striking qualities and the fact that the new production flowed out of the music and was not, as the first had been, imposed on it, Massine's composition had in places something forced and artificial about it. This defect frequently arises, as choreographers are fond of cutting up a rhythmic episode of the music into fragments, of working up each fragment separately, and then sticking the fragments together. By reason of this dissection, the choreographic line, which should coincide with that of the music, rarely does so, and the results are deplorable; the choreographer can never by such methods obtain a plastic rendering of the musical phrase. In putting together these small units (choreographical bars) he obtains, it is true, a total which agrees with the length of a given musical fragment, but he achieves nothing more, and the music is not adequately represented by a mere addition sum, but demands from choreography an organic equivalent of its own proportions. Moreover, this procedure on the part of the choreographer reacts unfavorably on the music itself, preventing the listener from recognizing the musical fragment choreographed. I speak from experience, because my music has frequently suffered from this deplorable method.

As Diaghileff's affairs were at this time in very low water financially, the reproduction of the *Sacre* had been made possible only by the backing of his friends. I should like especially to mention Mlle Gabrielle Chanel, who not only generously came to the assistance of the venture, but took an active part in the production by arranging to have the costumes made in her world-famous dressmaking establishment.

In the course of this Diaghileff season at the Théatre des Champs-Elysées I at last had an opportunity of seeing *Parade*, the work of Cocteau, Satie, and Picasso, the production of which in 1917 had been the subject of so much discussion. Although I had played the music on the piano, seen photographs of the scenery and costumes, and was intimately acquainted with the scenario, the performance gave me the impression of freshness and real originality. *Parade* confirmed me still further in my conviction of Satie's merit in the part he had played in French music by opposing to the vagueness of a decrepit impressionism a precise and firm language stripped of all pictorial embellishments.

In the spring of 1921 a Paris music hall asked me if I could let them have a few pages of incidental music for a little sketch, within the range of their audience. It amused me to try my hand at that sort of thing, and I therefore orchestrated four pieces taken from my collection of *Easy Duets*. Although my orchestra was more than modest, the composition as I wrote it was given only at the first few performances. When I went to see the sketch again a month later I found that there was but little left of what I had written. Everything was completely muddled; some instruments were lacking or had been replaced by others, and the music itself as executed by this pitiful band had become unrecognizable. It was a good lesson. One must never risk entrusting honest work to that sort of establishment in which music is certain to be mutilated to suit the show and its patrons.

Diaghileff was engaged for a season at the Royal Theatre, Madrid, in the spring, and asked me to go with him to conduct *Petroushka*, the King's favorite ballet. Alfonso and the two Queens came to all the performances, and, as usual, enjoyed them. They were present also at an informal party that the management of the Royal Theatre gave in our honor, and to which some of the artists of our company were also invited. Diaghileff and I decided to spend Easter at Seville, with its famous processions of *la Semana Santa*. Throughout those seven days we mingled with the crowds. It is astonishing that these fetes, half pagan, half Christian, and consecrated by time, have lost nothing of their freshness and vitality – notwithstanding the travel agencies and all the guides who are beyond price but have to be paid, and notwithstanding, moreover, the particular kind of publicity which has been their fate.

The spring and summer of 1921 were very much disturbed. First there was Diaghileff's Paris season, with the new production of *Le Sacre* and the creation of *Bouffon* (*Chout*), Prokofiev's masterpiece, which unfortunately one never hears now in its entirety. Then came my prolonged stay in London, where *Le Sacre* was given first at a concert conducted by Eugene Goossens and, later, at the theatre by the Diaghileff company.

Though it was terribly hot in London that summer, the town was very full, and I was constantly surrounded by friends and newly made acquaintances. It was one continuous round of lunches, teas, receptions, and weekends which left me no time to myself.

I cannot pass over in silence an event in this London visit which caused me a good deal of distress. Koussevitsky was giving a concert, and asked me to entrust him with the first performance of my *Symphonies d'Instruments à Vent à la Mémoire de Debussy*. I did not, and indeed I could not, count on any immediate success for this work. It is devoid of all the elements which infallibly appeal to the ordinary listener and to which he is accustomed. It would be futile to look in it for any passionate impulse or dynamic brilliance. It is an austere ritual which is unfolded in terms of short litanies between different groups of homogeneous instruments.

I fully anticipated that the *cantilène* of clarinets and flutes, frequently taking up again their liturgical dialogue and softly chanting it, did not offer sufficient attraction to a public which had so recently shown me their enthusiasm for the "revolutionary" *Sacre du Printemps*. This music is not meant "to please" an audience or to rouse its passions. I had hoped, however, that it would appeal to those in whom a purely musical receptivity outweighed the desire to satisfy emotional cravings. Alas! the conditions under which the work was given made that impossible. In the first place, it was given in an ill-chosen sequence. This music, composed for a score of wind instruments, an ensemble to which people were not accustomed at that time and whose timbre was bound to seem rather disappointing, was placed immediately after the pompous marches of the *Coq d'Or*, with their well-known orchestral brilliancy. And this is what happened: as soon as the marches were finished, three-quarters of the

95

instrumentalists left their seats, and in the vast arena of Queen's Hall I saw my twenty musicians still in their places at the back of the platform at an enormous distance from the conductor. The sight was peculiar in itself. To see a conductor gesticulating in front of an empty space, with all the more effort because the players were so far away, was somewhat disturbing. To conduct or control a group of instrumentalists at such a distance is an exceedingly arduous task. It was particularly arduous on this occasion, as the character of my music demanded the most delicate care to attain the ear of the public and to tame the audience to it. Both my work and Koussevitsky himself were thus victimized by untoward circumstances in which no conductor in the world could have made good.

The success of his season of the Ballet Russe made Diaghileff eager to realize a long-cherished project for the revival of the *chef d'oeuvre* of our classical ballet – Tchaikovsky's *Sleeping Beauty*. Knowing my great admiration for the composer, and that I entirely approved his idea, Diaghileff asked me to help him to carry out his plan. It was necessary to examine the score of the ballet, which had been obtained with the utmost difficulty, as it was, I believe, the only copy extant in Europe outside Russia. It was not even engraved. Certain parts which had been cut at its first production in St. Petersburg, and which Diaghileff wanted to include, were not in the orchestral score, but were to be found only in the pianoforte arrangement. I undertook to orchestrate them, and, as Diaghileff had himself reversed the order of various numbers, he asked me also to arrange the harmonic and orchestral connections needed.

During this same visit Diaghileff and I conceived another plan that I had very much at heart. What gave rise to it was our common love and admiration for our great poet

Pushkin, who for foreigners, alas! is but a name in an encyclopedia, but whose genius in all its versatility and universatility was not only particularly dear and precious to us, but represented a whole school of thought. By his nature, his mentality, and his ideology Pushkin was the most perfect representative of that wonderful line which began with Peter the Great and which, by a fortunate alloy, has united the most characteristically Russian elements with the spiritual riches of the West.

Diaghileff unquestionably belonged to this line, and all his activities have only confirmed the authenticity of that origin. As for myself, I had always been aware that I had in me the germs of this same mentality only needing development, and I subsequently deliberately cultivated them.

Was not the difference between this mentality and the mentality of the Five, which had so rapidly become academic and concentrated in the Belaieff circle under the domination of Rimsky-Korsakov and Glazounov, that the former was, as it were, cosmopolitan, whereas the latter was purely nationalist? The national element occupies a prominent place with Pushkin as well as with Glinka and Tchaikovsky. But with them it flows spontaneously from their very nature, whereas with the others the nationalistic tendency was a doctrinaire catechism they wished to impose. This nationalistic, ethnographical aesthetic which they persisted in cultivating was not in reality far removed from the spirit which inspired those films one sees of the old Russia of the tsars and boyars. What is so obvious in them, as indeed in the modern Spanish "folklorists," whether painters or musicians, is that naive but dangerous tendency which prompts them to remake an art that has already been created instinctively by the genius of the people. It is a sterile tendency and an evil from which many talented artists suffer.

97

It is true that Occidentalism was equally manifest in both the groups in question, but its origins were different.

Tchaikovsky, like Dargomijsky and others less well known, although using popular airs, did not hesitate to present them in a Gallicized or Italianized form in the manner of Glinka. The "nationalists" Europeanized their music just as much, but they were inspired by very different models – Wagner, Liszt, Berlioz – that is to say, by the spirit of romanticism and program music.

It is true that a Tchaikovsky could not escape Germanic influences. But, though he was under the influence of Schumann, that did not prevent him from remaining Russian any more than Gounod, for example, was prevented from remaining French. Both profited by the purely musical discoveries of the great German, who was himself so eminently a musician. They borrowed his phraseology and his distinctive idioms without adopting his ideology.

The project of which I spoke above resulted in the composition of my opera, *Mavra*, taken from Pushkin's rhymed story, *The Little House in Kolomna*. By this choice, about which Diaghileff and I were in complete agreement, I asserted my attitude towards the two trends of Russian thought between which I have just differentiated. On the musical plane this poem of Pushkin's led me straight to Glinka and Tchaikovsky, and I resolutely took up my position beside them. I thus clearly defined my tastes and predilections, my opposition to the contrary aesthetic, and assumed once more the good tradition established by these masters. Moreover, I dedicated my work to the memory of Pushkin, Glinka, and Tchaikovsky.

At the end of the summer I left London and went to Anglet, near Biarritz, to rejoin my family. There I began a task which enthralled me – a transcription for the piano which I called *Three Movements from Petroushka*. I wanted with this to provide piano virtuosi with a piece having sufficient scope to enable them to add to their modern repertory and display their technique. After that I began the composition of *Mavra*, for which a libretto in verse after Pushkin was being written by a young Russian poet, Boris Kochno. He sent me his text bit by bit as he wrote it. I liked his verse very much, and I appreciated his intelligence and his literary gifts and greatly enjoyed my work with him. Later he became one of Diaghileff's active collaborators.

With the approach of autumn I had temporarily to interrupt the work in order to devote myself to *The Sleeping Beauty*, which was to be produced very soon. When that was finished I went to London.

There I saw, as presented by Diaghileff, that *chef d'oeuvre* of Tchaikovsky and Petipa. Diaghileff had worked at it passionately and lovingly, and once more displayed his profound knowledge of the art of the ballet. He put all his soul, all his strength, into it, and in the most disinterested way, for there was here no question of enhancing his reputation as a pioneer or appealing to the curiosity of the public by new forms. In presenting something classical and dignified he demonstrated the greatness and freedom of his mentality together with a capacity to appreciate not only the values of today and of remote periods, but also – and this is an extremely rare quality – the values of the period immediately preceding our own.

It was a real joy to me to take part in this creation, not only for love of Tchaikovsky but also because of my profound admiration for classical ballet, which in its very essence, by the beauty of its *ordonnance* and the aristocratic austerity

99

of its forms, so closely corresponds with my conception of art. For here, in classical dancing, I see the triumph of studied conception over vagueness, of the rule over the arbitrary, of order over the haphazard. I am thus brought face to face with the eternal conflict in art between the Apollonian and the Dionysian principles. The latter assumes ecstasy to be the final goal – that is to say, the losing of oneself – whereas art demands above all the full consciousness of the artist. There can, therefore, be no doubt as to my choice between the two. And if I appreciate so highly the value of classical ballet, it is not simply a matter of taste on my part, but because I see exactly in it the perfect expression of the Apollonian principle.

The first performances of *The Sleeping Beauty*, the lavish setting of which had been created by Leon Bakst, had a brilliant success, and the public thronged to it. Unfortunately, the enormous sums invested in the undertaking compelled the theatrical management to continue its run for months, until at last there were not enough people left to fill the theatre, and it became necessary to withdraw it. But the last night, as I learned later, was a veritable triumph; the audience would not go away, and there was great difficulty in emptying the building.

VII

After the first few performances I returned to Biarritz, where I settled with my family and where we stayed for the next three years. There I worked all the winter at *Mavra*.

It was at this time that my connection with the Pleyel Company began. They had suggested that I should make a transcription of my works for their Pleyela mechanical piano.

My interest in the work was twofold. In order to prevent the distortion of my compositions by future interpreters, I had always been anxious to find a means of imposing some restriction on the notorious liberty, especially widespread today, which prevents the public from obtaining a correct idea of the author's intentions. This possibility was now afforded by the rolls of the mechanical piano, and, a little later, by gramophone records.

The means enabled me to determine for the future the relationships of the movements (*tempi*) and the nuances in accordance with my wishes. It is true that this guaranteed nothing, and in the ten years which have since elapsed I have, alas! had ample opportunity of seeing how ineffective it has proved in practice. But these transcriptions nevertheless enabled me to create a lasting document which should be of service to those executants who would rather know and follow my intentions than stray into irresponsible interpretations of my musical text.

There was a second direction in which this work gave me satisfaction. This was not simply the reduction of an orchestral work to the limitations of a piano of seven octaves. It was the process of adaptation to an instrument which had, on the one hand, unlimited possibilities of precision, velocity, and polyphony, but which, on the other hand, constantly presented serious difficulties in establishing dynamic relationships. These tasks developed and exercised my imagination by constantly presenting new problems of an instrumental nature closely connected with the questions of acoustics, harmony, and part writing.

It was a restless winter for me, as I had to travel a good deal. My work at Pleyel's entailed frequent visits to Paris, and I had to attend the rehearsals of *Mavra* and *Renard*, which were just going to be produced by Diaghileff at the Paris Opera House, thanks to the generous help of Princess Edmond de Polignac.

This necessitated several visits to Monte Carlo, where the choreography of *Renard* was being created by Bronislava Nijinska, sister of the famous dancer and herself an excellent dancer endowed with a profoundly artistic nature, and, in contrast to her brother, gifted with a real talent for choreographic creation.

Diaghileff and I also confided to her the direction of the artists acting in *Mavra* as regards plastic movement. She had marvelous ideas, which were unfortunately balked by the inability of the singers to subject themselves to a technique and discipline in the practice of which they were unversed.

It was quite different with *Renard*. I still deeply regret that the production, which gave me the greatest satisfaction both musically (the music was under the direction of Ansermet) and scenically (the scenery and costumes were by Larionov and were one of his greatest successes), has never been revived in that form. Nijinska had admirably seized the spirit of its montebank buffoonery. She displayed such a wealth of ingenuity, so many fine points, and so much satirical verve that the effect was irresistible. She herself, playing the part of *Renard*, created an unforgettable figure.

Mavra had its first concert production at a soiree given by Diaghileff at the Hôtel Continental. I myself accompanied it at the piano. The first performance of *Mavra* and *Renard* at the Paris Opera was on June 3, 1922.

Alas! I was deeply disappointed by the disastrous surroundings in which my poor *Mavra* and little *Renard* found themselves. Being a part of a Ballet Russe program, my two intimate acts were dwarfed when sandwiched between spectacular pieces which formed the repertory of Diaghileff's season and were the special attraction for the general public. This crushing environment, the enormous framework of the opera house, and also the mentality of the audience, composed mainly of the famous *abonnés*, all combined to make my two little pieces, especially *Mavra*, seem out of place. Though very conscientiously executed by the Polish conductor Fitelberg, alternating at that time with Ansermet in the repertory of the Ballet Russe, *Mavra* was regarded as a disconcerting freak of mine, and a downright failure. Such was also the attitude of all the critics, notably those of the pre-war left. They condemned the whole thing then and there, attaching no importance to it, and regarding it as unworthy of closer examination. Only a few musicians of the younger generation appreciated *Mavra*, and realized that it marked a turning point in the evolution of my musical thought.

For my own part, I was glad to see that I had completely succeeded in realizing my musical ideas, and was therefore encouraged to develop them further – this time in the domain of symphony. I began to compose my *Octuor pour Instruments à Vent*.

I began to write this music without knowing what its sound medium would be – that is to say, what instrumental form it would take. I only decided that point after finishing the first part, when I saw clearly what ensemble was demanded by the contrapuntal material, the character, and structure of what I had composed.

My special interest in wind instruments in various combinations had been roused when I was composing *Symphonies à la Mémoire de Debussy*, and this interest had continued to grow during the ensuing period. Thus, after I had, in these *Symphonies*, used the ordinary wind orchestra (wood and brass), I added in *Mavra* double basses and violoncellos and, episodically, a little trio of two violins and viola.

Having again used a wind ensemble for chamber music in the *Octuor*, I later undertook the composition of my *Concerto*, which, as regards color, is yet another combination – that of piano with a wind orchestra reinforced by double basses and timbals.

But in speaking of the *Concerto* I have deliberately somewhat overstepped the chronological order of my narrative to let the reader see the line of investigation that I was pursuing at that period, which, looking back now after many years, seems to have constituted a marked epoch in my creative activity.

This preoccupation with the subject of tone material manifested itself also in my instrumentation of *Les Noces*, which, after long delays, was at last to be produced by Diaghileff.

While still at Morges I had tried out various forms of instrumentation, first of all for a large orchestra, which I gave up almost at once in view of the elaborate apparatus that the complexity of that form demanded. I next sought for a solution in a smaller ensemble. I began a score which required massed polyphonic effects: a mechanical piano and an electrically driven harmonium, a section of percussion instruments, and two Hungarian cymbalons. But there I was balked by a fresh obstacle, namely, the great difficulty for the conductor of synchronizing the parts executed by instrumentalists and singers with those rendered by the mechanical players. I was thus compelled to abandon this idea also, although I had already orchestrated the first two scenes in that way, work which had demanded a great deal of strength and patience, but which was all pure loss.

I did not touch *Les Noces* again for nearly four years, so busy was I with more urgent matters, and Diaghileff put off its production from year to year.

It was at last decided that it should be staged at the beginning of June, 1923, and Diaghileff asked me to help Bronislava Nijinska with the rehearsals of her choreography at Monte Carlo in March and April. But the essential thing was to find a solution for the instrumental ensemble, and that I kept putting off in the hope that it would come of itself when the definite fixing of a date for the first performance should make it imperative. And that, in fact, is what happened. I saw clearly that the sustained, that is to say *soufflé* elements (*the elements produced by the breath, as the "wind" in an instrument ensemble*) in my work would be best supported by an ensemble consisting exclusively of percussion instruments. I thus found my solution in the form of an orchestra comprising piano, timbals, bells, and xylophones, none of which instruments gives a precise note.

Such a sound combination in *Les Noces* was the necessary outcome of the music itself, and it was in nowise suggested by a desire to imitate the sounds of popular fetes of this kind, which I had, indeed, neither seen nor heard. It was in this spirit, too, that I had composed my music without borrowing anything from folk music with the exception of the theme of a factory song which I used several times in the last scene, with different words ("I have gold that hangs down to my waist"; "The beautiful well-made bed, the beautiful square bed"). All the other themes, airs, and melodies were of my own invention.

I set myself to work on the instrumentation at the end of the winter, while still at Biarritz, and I finished it on April 6 at Monaco. I must say that the stage production of *Les Noces*, though obviously one of talent, did not correspond with my original plan. I had pictured to myself something quite different.

According to my idea, the spectacle should have been a *divertissement*, and that is what I wanted to call it. It was not my intention to reproduce the ritual of peasant weddings, and I paid little heed to ethnographical considerations. My idea was to compose a sort of scenic ceremony, using as I liked those ritualistic elements so abundantly provided by village customs which had been established for centuries in the celebration of Russian marriages. I took my inspiration from those customs, but reserved to myself the right to use them with absolute freedom. Inspired by the same reasons as in *L'Histoire d'un Soldat*, I wanted all my instrumental apparatus to be visible side by side with the actors or dancers, making it, so to speak, a participant in the whole theatrical action. For this reason, I wished to place the orchestra on the stage itself, letting the actors move on the space remaining free. The fact that the artists in the scene would uniformly wear costumes of a Russian character while the musicians would be in evening dress not only did not embarrass me, but, on the contrary, was perfectly in keeping with my idea of a *divertissement* of the masquerade type.

But Diaghileff had no sympathy with my wishes. And when, to convince him, I pointed out how successful the plan had been in *L'Histoire d'un Soldat*, I only stimulated his furious resistance because he could not bear *L'Histoire*.

106

So all my efforts in that direction were vain, and as I did not feel that I had a right to jeopardize the performance since, after all, the scenic realization did not compromise my work, I very reluctantly consented to Diaghileff's staging.

The first performance of *Les Noces* was given on June 13, 1923, at the Théatre de la Gaîté Lyrique in Paris. It was admirably conducted by Ansermet, and became one of the most remarkable triumphs of his conducting.

The framework of the *décor* was composed exclusively of backcloths, with just a few details of a Russian peasant cottage interior, and both coloring and lighting were very successful. Natalie Goncharova was responsible for it, and also for the costumes very ingeniously simplified and made uniform.

The first night of *Les Noces* had been preceded by a private audition in concert form at the house of Princess Edmond de Polignac, who never missed an opportunity of showing me her affection and sympathy. An excellent musician, of wide culture, a painter endowed with undeniable talent, she encouraged and was the patron of artists and the arts. I shall always gratefully remember the evenings at her house where I played several of my new creations, such as – besides *Les Noces* – *L'Histoire d'un Soldat*, my *Concerto*, my piano *Sonate* (which is dedicated to her), *Oedipus Rex*, and so forth.

In August of that same year I went on a short visit to Weimar, at the invitation of the organizers of a very fine exhibition of modern architecture (*Bauhaus*), in the course of which there was a series of musical performances, including, among other things, the presentation of my *L'Histoire d'un Soldat*. It had already been given in Germany, two months earlier, at Frankfort-on-Main, at one of seven concerts of modern music (*Neue Kammermusik*) organized in that city with the help of Paul Hindemith.

My journey to Weimar was something of an adventure. In Paris I could not get a through ticket. All I could obtain was a ticket to the station where the zone of occupation began, a little way from Frankfort. It was quite late when I reached the little station, which was occupied by African soldiers with fixed bayonets. I was told that at that hour there was no means of communication with Frankfort, and that I must wait till daylight, contenting myself till then with the bench in the waiting room, which was, moreover, already crowded to overflowing. I wanted at first to look for a bed in the village, but was warned that it would be risky to go out in the dark because of the vigilance of the sentries, who might mistake me for a vagrant. It was so dark that I had to abandon the idea and stay at the station, counting the hours till dawn. It was not till 7 A.M. that, guided by a child, and after a tramp of half an hour along rain-soaked roads, I finally reached the shelter of the tram which took me to the central station of Frankfort, where I found a train to Weimar.

I have retained one memory, which is particularly dear to me, of my short stay at Weimar, where the *Soldat* was very warmly received by the public. I made the acquaintance of Ferruccio Busoni, whom I had never met before and who had always been described to me as an irreconcilable opponent of my music. I was therefore very much impressed by the sincere emotion that I saw he was feeling while my music was being played, which was confirmed by him that same evening. I was all the more touched by this appreciation, since it came from a very great musician, whose work and mentality were fundamentally opposed to the spirit of my art. It was my first and last sight of him; he died a year later.

I must come back now to my *Octuor*, the composition of which had been interrupted while I was orchestrating *Les Noces*. I finished it in May, 1923, and conducted it myself on October 18 of that year in the Paris Opera House at a Koussevitzky concert.

I remember what an effort it cost me to establish an ensemble of eight wind instruments, for they could not strike the listener's ear with a great display of tone. In order that this music should reach the ear of the public it was necessary to emphasize the entries of the several instruments, to introduce breathing spaces between the phrases (rests), to pay particular care to the intonation, the instrumental prosody, the accentuation – in short, to establish order and discipline in the purely sonorous scheme to which I always give precedence over elements of an emotional character. It was all the more difficult because at that time, when I was only just beginning my career as a conductor, I had not yet got the necessary technique, which I acquired later only with practice. And, for that matter, the instrumentalists themselves were unaccustomed to this method of treating the art of playing because, all told, very few conductors employ it.

In January I went to Antwerp, having been invited by La Société des Nouveaux Concerts to conduct a program of my earlier works. From there I went to Brussels, where the Pro Arte Society had organized a concert of my music. The celebrated Quartet – known under that name (MM. A. Onnou, L. Halleux, G. Prévost, and R. Maas) – with its usual masterly seriousness played my *Concertino* and my *Trois Petites Pièces pour Quatuor à Cordes*, while I myself conducted my *Octuor*, *La Suite de Pulcinella*, and my opera *Mavra*, the vocal parts of which had been carefully studied and prepared by the singers before my arrival with the help of that enthusiastic Belgian musician, Paul Collaer. I give all these details because I retain a grateful memory of the Pro Arte group for this concert, organized in a highly artistic fashion, which enabled me to present my work, especially *Mavra*, under conditions which I could not have wished better.

In this connection I must mention here the first concert performance of *Mavra* a year earlier. Jean Wiener, who had at that time arranged a series of auditions of contemporary music in Paris, on December 26, 1922, gave a concert consisting exclusively of my music, including my *Symphonies pour Instruments à Vent* and *Mavra*, conducted by Ansermet. This time also the conditions provided were those which are essential if the music is to be heard and appreciated by the public.

My visit to Belgium had prevented me from going to Monte Carlo, where Diaghileff was then giving a season of French operas which we had selected together, and to the production of which he devoted the utmost care. In the winter of 1922–1923 I often went to the small Trianon Lyrique, a modest and charming theatre of long standing. Louis Masson, its director, was a serious musician and excellent conductor, with a firm baton and very fine taste. He gave unpretentious performances there which were perfectly executed. He deserves gratitude for the courage with which he put on works of high musical value which the official theatres had, alas! cast aside as old-fashioned and no longer attractive to the general public. This attitude of the great theatres is all the more deplorable in that, while depriving well-informed musicians of infallible enjoyment, it lets slip an opportunity for educating the public and directing their taste in a favorable direction. For my own part, I took great pleasure in these performances, especially Cimarosa's *Secret Mariage* and Gounod's *Philémon et Baucis*. In hearing this latter opera I once again experienced the charm which emanates from the intimate aroma of Gounod's music. Diaghileff was as much in love with it as I was, and this gave us the idea of looking through his works in the hope of finding forgotten pieces.

We thus discovered the short but delicious comic opera, *La Colombe*, written for the theatre at Baden-Baden in the reign of Napoleon III, and we found also that little masterpiece, *Le Médecin Malgré Lui*. Diaghileff also happened to run across *L'Education Manquée*, a charming piece by Chabrier. His great importance is still not fully appreciated by his own compatriots, who persist in treating him with kindly indulgence, seeing in him nothing more than an amusing and lively amateur. It is clear that ears corrupted by emotional and sentimental verbiage, and inoculated with academic doctrine (which, however, is less serious), cannot but remain deaf to the quality of such a real pearl as *Le Médecin Malgré Lui*, which has against it the misfortune of being purely music.

As I said before, I had not had a chance of seeing the Gounod operas which Diaghileff was producing at Monte Carlo. I know only that the public had proved indifferent to those performances and had not appreciated my friend's gesture. In their uncultured snobbishness the greatest fear of these people was lest they should appear to be behind the times if they showed enjoyment for music stupidly condemned by the publicity-mongers of what was once the advance guard. I was myself a witness of this foolish attitude of the public at the first performance of *L'Education Manquée* during the Russian Ballet season at the Champs-Elysées. The title was ironic, for the audience displayed a complete lack of education. Being accustomed to see nothing but ballets at Diaghileff's performances, they considered that they were swindled in having to see an opera, however short, and indicated their impatience by interruptions and cries of "Dance, dance." It was nauseating. It is only fair to say that these interruptions came for the most part from outsiders, who were easily recognized as such by their foreign accent. And to think that this same audience listens devoutly and with angelic patience to the edifying harangues of King Mark endlessly reiterated at official gala performances under the baton of some star conductor!

Side by side with forgotten works, Diaghileff had wanted to present in that season the music of composers belonging to the young French school, by giving ballets which he had commissioned from them. These included Georges Auric's *Les Fâcheux*, the music of which is full of verve and pungency, with the unforgettable scenery and costumes by Georges Braque; Francis Poulenc's youthful and tender *Biches*, in the delicate framework designed by Marie Laurencin; and finally, *Le Train Bleu* by Darius Milhaud, with its lively sporting pace. The admirably successful choreography of these three ballets came from Bronislava Nijinska's inexhaustible talent. The performance was brilliant, and it gives me great pleasure to mention here such admirable executants as Vera Nemtchinova, Leon Woizikovsky, and Anton Dolin.

VIII

My concerts in Belgium, followed in March by several at Barcelona and Madrid, mark, so to speak, the beginning of my career as executant of my own works. In fact I had that year a whole series of engagements in various towns in Europe and the United States, and had not only to conduct my own compositions, but also to play my *Concerto* for piano and orchestra, which I had just finished.

While on this subject, I ought to say that the idea of playing my *Concerto* myself was suggested by Koussevitzky, who happened to be at Biarritz when I was finishing its composition. I hesitated at first, fearing that I should not have time to perfect my technique as a pianist, to practice enough, and to acquire the endurance necessary to execute a work demanding sustained effort. But as I am by nature always tempted by anything needing prolonged effort, and prone to persist in overcoming difficulties, and as, also, the prospect of creating my work for myself, and thus establishing the manner in which I wished it to be played, greatly attracted me, these influences combined to induce me to undertake it.

I began, therefore, the loosening of my fingers by playing a lot of Czerny exercises, which was not only very useful but gave me keen musical pleasure. I have always admired Czerny, not only as a remarkable teacher but also as a thoroughbred musician.

While learning by heart the piano part of my *Concerto*, I had simultaneously to accustom myself to keep in mind and hear the various parts of the orchestra, so that my attention should not be distracted while I was playing. For a novice like myself this was hard work, to which I had to devote many hours every day.

My first public performance of the *Concerto* took place at the Paris Opera on May 22 at a Koussevitzky concert, after I had played it a week earlier to an intimate gathering at the Princess de Polignac's with Jean Wiener playing the accompaniment on a piano.

At the beginning of my career as a piano soloist I naturally suffered from stage fright, and for a long time I had a good deal of difficulty in overcoming it. It was only by habit and sustained effort that I managed, in time, to master my nerves and so to withstand one of the most distressing sensations that I know. In analyzing the cause of this stage fright, I have come to the conclusion that it is chiefly due to fear of a lapse of memory or of some distraction, however trifling, which might have irreparable consequences. For the slightest gap, even a mere wavering, risks giving rise to a fatal discordance between the piano and the orchestral body, which obviously cannot, in any circumstances, hold the movement of its own part in suspense. I remember at my first debut being seized by just such a lapse of memory, though it fortunately had no dire results. Having finished the first part of my *Concerto*, just before beginning the Largo which opens with a piano solo, I suddenly realized that I had entirely forgotten how it started. I whispered this to Koussevitsky. He glanced at the score and whispered the first notes. That was enough to restore my balance and enable me to attack the Largo.

Incidentally, I must mention a flying visit that I paid to Copenhagen, such a cheerful town in summer, which I went to several times later, and always with the same pleasure. I played my *Concerto* at the Tivoli at one of the summer season symphony concerts.

When I returned to Biarritz I had to arrange our removal to Nice, where I had decided to live, because the Atlantic gales got on my nerves, especially in winter. The last few months of my stay at Biarritz were devoted to the composition of my *Sonate pour Piano*.

After the *Octuor* and the *Concerto*, my interest was

114

completely and continuously absorbed in thoughts of instrumental music pure and simple, untrammeled by any scenic consideration. The recent task of writing the piano parts of my *Concerto* and *Noces* had greatly stimulated my keenness for that instrument. I therefore decided to compose a piece for pianoforte solo in several movements. This was my *Sonate*. I gave it that name without, however, giving it the classical form such as we find it in Clementi, Haydn, Mozart, which as everyone knows, is conditioned by the allegro. I used the term sonata in its original meaning – deriving from *sonare*, in contrast to *cantare*, whence *cantata*. In using the term, therefore, I did not regard myself as restricted by any predetermined form.

But, though determined to retain full liberty in composing this work, I had, while engaged on it, a strong desire to examine more closely the sonatas of the classical masters in order to trace the direction and development of their thought in the solution of the problems presented by that form.

I therefore replayed, among others, a great many of Beethoven's sonatas. In our early youth we were surfeited by his works, his famous *Weltschmerz* being forced upon us at the same time, together with his "tragedy" and all the commonplace utterances voiced for more than a century about this composer who must be recognized as one of the world's greatest musical geniuses.

Like many other musicians, I was disgusted by this intellectual and sentimental attitude, which had little to do with serious musical appreciation. This deplorable pedagogy did not fail in its result. It alienated me from Beethoven for many years.

Cured and matured by age, I could now approach him

objectively so that he wore a different aspect for me. Above all I recognized in him the indisputable monarch of the instrument. It is the instrument that inspires his thought and determines its substance. The relations of a composer to his sound medium may be of two kinds. Some, for example, compose music *for* the piano; others compose *piano music*. Beethoven is clearly in the second category. In all his immense pianistic work, it is the "instrumental" side which is characteristic of him and makes him infinitely precious to me. It is the giant instrumentalist that predominates in him, and it is thanks to that quality that he cannot fail to reach any ear that is open to music.

But is it in truth Beethoven's music which has inspired the innumerable works devoted to this prodigious musician by thinkers, moralists, and even sociologists who have suddenly become musicographers? In this connection I should like to quote the following passage taken from an article in the great Soviet daily, *Izvestia*:

"Beethoven is the friend and the contemporary of the French Revolution, and he remained faithful to it even at the time when, during the Jacobin dictatorship, humanitarians with weak nerves of the Schiller type turned from it, preferring to destroy tyrants on the theatrical stage with the help of cardboard swords. Beethoven, that plebian genius, who proudly turned his back on emperors, princes, and magnates – that is the Beethoven we love for his unassailable optimism, his virile sadness, for the inspired pathos of his struggle, and for his iron will which enabled him to seize destiny by the throat."

This *chef d'oeuvre* of penetration comes from the pen of one of the most famous of the musical critics of the U.S.S.R. I should like to know in what this mentality differs from the platitudes and commonplace utterances of the publicity-mongers of liberalism in all the bourgeois democracies long before the social revolution in Russia.

I do not mean to say that everything that has been written on Beethoven in this sense is of the same quality. But, in the majority of these works, do not the panegyrists base their adulation far more on the sources of his inspiration than on the music itself? Could they have filled their fat volumes if they had not been able to embroider to their hearts' content all the extramusical elements available in the Beethoven life and legend, drawing their conclusions and judgments on the artist from them?

What does it matter whether the *Third Symphony* was inspired by the figure of Bonaparte the Republican or Napoleon the Emperor? It is only the music that matters. But to talk music is risky, and entails responsibility. Therefore some find it preferable to seize on side issues. It is easy, and enables you to pass as a deep thinker.

This reminds me of the account of a conversation between Mallarmé and Degas which I had from Paul Valéry. Degas, who, as is well known, liked to dabble in poetry, one day said to Mallarmé: "I cannot manage the end of my sonnet, and it is not that I am wanting in ideas." Mallarmé, softly: "It is not with ideas that one makes sonnets, but with words."

So it is with Beethoven. It is in the quality of his musical material and not in the nature of his ideas that his true greatness lies.

It is time that this was recognized, and Beethoven was rescued from the unjustifiable monopoly of the "intellectuals" and left to those who seek in music for nothing but music. It is, however, also time – and this is perhaps even more urgent – to protect him from the stupidity and drivel of fools who think it up to date to giggle as they amuse themselves by running him down. Let them beware; dates pass quickly.

Just as in his pianistic work Beethoven lives on the piano, so, in his symphonies, overtures, and chamber music he draws his sustenance from his instrumental ensemble. With him the instrumentation is never apparel, and that is why it never strikes one. The profound wisdom with which he distributes parts to separate instruments or to whole groups, the carefulness of his instrumental writing, and the precision with which he indicates his wishes – all these testify to the fact that we are above all in the presence of a tremendous constructive force.

I do not think that I am mistaken in asserting that it was just his manner of molding his musical material which logically led to the erection of those monumental structures which are his supreme glory.

There are those who contend that Beethoven's instrumentation was bad and his tone color poor. Others altogether ignore that side of his art, holding that instrumentation is a secondary matter and that only "ideas" are worthy of consideration.

The former demonstrate their lack of taste, their complete incompetence in this respect, and their narrow and mischievous mentality. In contrast with the florid orchestration of Wagner, with its lavish coloring, Beethoven's instrumentation will appear to lack luster. It might produce a similar impression if compared with the vivacious radiance of Mozart. But Beethoven's music is intimately linked up with his instrumental language, and finds its most exact and perfect expression in the sobriety of that language. To regard it as poverty-stricken would merely show lack of perception. True sobriety is a great rarity, and most difficult of attainment.

As for those who attach no importance to Beethoven's instrumentation, but ascribe the whole of his greatness to his "ideas" – they obviously regard all instrumentation as a mere matter of apparel, coloring, flavoring, and so fall, though following a different path, into the same heresy as the others.

Both make the same fundamental error of regarding instrumentation as something extrinsic from the music for which it exists.

This dangerous point of view concerning instrumentation, coupled with the unhealthy greed for orchestral opulence of today, has corrupted the judgment of the public, and they, being impressed by the immediate effect of tone color, can no longer solve the problem of whether it is intrinsic in the music or simply "padding." Orchestration has become a source of enjoyment independent of the music, and the time has surely come to put things in their proper places. We have had enough of this orchestral dappling and these thick sonorities; one is tired of being saturated with timbres, and wants no more of all this overfeeding, which deforms the entity of the instrumental element by swelling it out of all proportion and giving it an existence of its own. There is a great deal of re-education to be accomplished in this field.

All these ideas were germinating in me while I was composing my sonata and once more renewing my contact with Beethoven. Their development has continued from that time to this, and my mind is full of them.

I had hardly settled down in the Riviera when I had to undertake a concert tour in central Europe. I went first to Warsaw and Prague; then to Leipzig and Berlin, where I played my *Concerto*, accompanied by Furtwängler. I also gave a concert at the Blüthersaal in Berlin, where, among other things, I conducted my *Octuor*. After that I went to Holland. I was hospitably welcomed at the Concertgebouw of Amsterdam by its eminent conductor Willem Mengelberg, and I played my *Concerto* under his direction at a concert, repeated two days later at The Hague, and shared the conductor's baton with him on another occasion.

Then I went to Geneva and to Lausanne to conduct my own compositions and to play under the direction of Ansermet. I finished my circuit with a concert at Marseilles.

I had to leave Europe soon afterwards for a comparatively long time, as I had signed a contract for a concert tour of two months in the United States. It was my first crossing of the Atlantic.

Without stopping to describe my visual impressions on landing in New York – skyscrapers, traffic, lights, Negroes, cinemas, theatres, in fact all that rouses the curiosity of foreigners, and very rightly so – I want to begin by bearing witness as a musician to the fact that in the United States, side by side with a pronounced weakness for the freakish and the sensational, I found a real taste for the art of music, as manifested by the many societies devoted to musical culture and by the magnificent orchestras munificently endowed by private individuals. In this respect the United States reminded me of Germany and Russia. I received the warmest and most hospitable welcome from musical societies, amateurs, and patrons, notably from Clarence H. Mackay, at whose invitation I had gone and who was at that time president of the New York Philharmonic.

The public was already acquainted with my most frequently performed works, which they had heard in many concerts, but what was a novelty was to see me in the roles of pianist and conductor. Judging by the full houses and the acclamations which I received, I flattered myself that I had achieved an undoubted success. But at that time it might have been ascribed to the attraction of novelty. It is only now, after my recent tour in that country, that I am convinced of the solid foundation on which the American public's interest in my music rests.

This time, morever, I was fully conscious of the approval of my manner of rendering my works even by critics accustomed to new-fangled conducting. I was glad that my ten years of effort in acquiring the proficiency necessary to present my works in the way I desired was rewarded by the public understanding of it. The serious interest of the Americans in music is displayed, among other ways, in the judicious selection of those to whom they apply for instruction. A large number of young people have come to France to complete their musical education – indeed, since the war this has become almost a tradition – and have found invaluable teachers in Nadia Boulanger and Isidore Philipp. I had the pleasure of meeting a whole series of their pupils, some performers and some teachers themselves, all musicians of solid knowledge and unerring taste, who, on returning to their own country, were engaged in spreading the excellent musical culture which they had acquired under these eminent masters, and in successfully combating pernicious influences and base amateurishness.

I hope some day to have an opportunity of saying more about this second visit to the United States, and to express more fully my sympathy with, and cordial attachment to, this new, hardy, naive, yet immense country.

Returning to my first tour in 1925, I will briefly enumerate the towns I visited. I began my itinerary with the New York Philharmonic, where I conducted in several con-

certs and played my *Concerto* under the direction of Mengelberg, as, later, I played in Boston under Koussevitzky, and
in Chicago, under the veteran Stock. Then followed Philadelphia, Cleveland, Detroit, and Cincinnati.

I retain a vivid and grateful memory of Chicago. My
friend Carpenter and his now lamented wife Rue gave me
the warmest of welcomes, and arranged a dinner in my
honor, which was followed by a concert of chamber music
at the Arts Club of which Mrs. Carpenter was president.

As I was under an engagement to play my *Concerto* at
the Philadelphia Orchestra, it was necessary for me to return
to that city, and in somewhat unusual circumstances. Having
been detained in the country, I could not reach Philadelphia
until the afternoon of the very day of my concert. Moreover,
the guest conductor, Fritz Reiner, of Cincinnati, who was to
accompany me in place of Leopold Stokowski, who was away
just then, had barely time to rehearse the program for the
evening, as he himself had arrived only that morning. Most
conductors devote several rehearsals to the preparation of
my *Concerto*, but on this occasion we had barely half an hour.
And there was a miracle. There was not a single hitch. It was
as though Reiner had played it time and again with that
orchestra. Such an extraordinary phenomenon could never
have occurred, notwithstanding the prodigious technique of
the conductor and the high quality of the orchestra, if
Reiner had not acquired a perfect knowledge of my score,
which he had procured some time before. One could aptly
apply to him the familiar saying: he has the score in his head
and not his head in the score.

I have told this little story to show that in America are
to be found musicians of the highest rank, such as Fritz
Reiner, whose value ought to be far more highly appreciated

than it is. But they are relegated to the background, over-shadowed by the fame and bulk of celebrated orchestral "stars" for whom the public evinces herd enthusiasm, failing to note that their aim is to outshine one another in the pursuit of personal triumphs, and generally at the expense of the music.

As soon as I returned to Europe, I had to go to Barcelona to conduct a festival of three concerts devoted to my music. On my arrival I had an amusing surprise, which I shall never forget. Among those who came to meet me at the station there was a very likable little journalist who, in interviewing me, carried his amiability to the pitch of saying, "Barcelona awaits you with impatience. Ah, if you only knew how we love your *Scheherazade* and your *Danses du Prince Igor!*" I had not the heart to undeceive him.

Another festival of my music was given in April at the Augusteo in Rome, under the direction of Molinari, at which I played my *Concerto*, and where the excellent vocalist, Mme Vera Janacopoulos, sang at a concert of chamber music under my direction.

When I returned to Paris in May, I conducted my *Ragtime* at the Opera and replayed my *Concerto* at a Koussevitzky concert of my compositions. After having seen the performances of the Ballet Russe, which had put on *Pulcinella* and the *Chant du Rossignol* in a new version by Massine, I returned to Nice for the summer months, to rest after my many journeys and to devote myself afresh to composition.

In America I had arranged with a gramophone firm to make records of some of my music. This suggested the idea that I should compose something whose length should be determined by the capacity of the record. I should in that way avoid all the trouble of cutting and adapting. And that is how my *Sérénade en* LA *pour Piano* came to be written. I had started it as early as April, beginning with the last portion, and now at Nice resumed its composition. The four movements constituting the piece are united under the title Sérénade, in imitation of the *Nachtmustk* of the eighteenth century, which was usually commissioned by patron princes for various festive occasions, and included, as did the suites, an indeterminate number of pieces.

Whereas these compositions were written for ensembles of instruments of greater or less importance, I wanted to condense mine into a small number of movements for one polyphonic instrument. In these pieces I represented some of the most typical moments of this kind of musical fete. I began with a solemn entry, a sort of hymn; this I followed by a solo of ceremonial homage paid by the artist to the guests; the third part, rhythmical and sustained, took the place of the various kinds of dance music intercalated in accordance with the manner of the serenades and suites of the period; and I ended with a sort of epilogue which was tantamount to an ornate signature with numerous carefully inscribed flourishes. I had a definite purpose in calling my composition *Sérénade en* LA. The title does not refer to its tonality, but to the fact that I had made all the music revolve about an axis of sound which happened to be the LA.

Working at this did not tire me much, and did not prevent me from enjoying a rest which I felt that I deserved, and which included various amusements, mainly that of motoring about the Riviera.

As soon as my *Sérénade* was finished I felt the necessity for undertaking something big. I had in mind an opera or an oratorio on some universally familiar subject. My idea was that in that way I could concentrate the whole attention of the audience, undistracted by the story, on the music itself, which would thus become both word and action.

With my thoughts full of this project, I started for Venice, where I had been invited to play my *Sonate* at the festival of the Société Internationale pour la Musique Contemporaine. I took advantage of this opportunity to make a little tour of Italy before returning to Nice. My last stopping-place was Genoa, and there I happened to find in a bookseller's a volume by Joergensen on St. Francis of Assisi of which I had already heard. In reading it I was struck by a passage which confirmed one of my most deeprooted convictions. It is common knowledge that the familiar speech of the saint was Provençal, but that on solemn occasions, such as prayer, he used French. I have always considered that a special language, and not that of current converse, was required for subjects touching on the sublime. That is why I was trying to discover what language would be most appropriate for my projected work, and why I finally selected Latin. The choice had the great advantage of giving me a medium not dead, but turned to stone and so monumentalized as to have become immune from all risk of vulgarization.

On my return my mind continued to dwell on my new work, and I decided to take my subject from the familiar myths of ancient Greece. I thought that I could not do better for my libertto than to appeal to my old friend, Jean Cocteau, of whom I saw a good deal, as he was then living not far from Nice. I had been frequently attracted by the idea of collaborating with him. I recall that at one time or another we had sketched out various plans but something had always arisen to prevent their materialization. I had just seen his *Antigone*, and had been much struck by the manner in which he had handled the ancient myth and presented it in modern guise. Cocteau's stagecraft is excellent. He has a sense of values and an eye and feeling for detail which always become of primary importance with him. This applies alike to the movements of the actors, the setting, the costumes, and, indeed, all the accessories. In the preceding year, too, I had again had an opportunity of appreciating these qualities of Cocteau in *La Machine Infernale*, in which his efforts were so ably seconded by the fine talent of Christian Bérard, who was responsible for the scenery.

For two months I was in constant touch with Cocteau. He was delighted with my idea, and set to work at once. We were in complete agreement in choosing *Oedipus Rex* as the subject. We kept our plans secret, wishing to give Diaghileff a surprise for the twentieth anniversary of his theatrical activities, which was to be celebrated in the spring of 1927.

Leaving Cocteau to his task, I undertook another concert tour at the beginning of November. I went first to Zurich to play my *Concerto* under the direction of Dr. Volkmar Andreae. At Basle I played it under that of the late Hermann Suter. From there I made a lightning visit to Winterthur, at the invitation of my friend Werner Reinhart, at whose house I played, among other things, my first suite for violin and piano from *Pulcinella* with that excellent young violinist, Alma Moodie.

I then went to Wiesbaden to take part as soloist in my *Concerto* at a symphony concert conducted by Klemperer. It was there that I got into touch for the first time with this eminent conductor, with whom later I so frequently had the opportunity and pleasure of working. I shall always retain a grateful and affectionate memory of our relations, for I found in Klemperer not only a devoted propagandist of my work, but a forceful conductor, with a generous nature and intelligence enough to realize that in closely following the author's directions there is no danger of prejudicing one's own individuality.

After a concert of chamber music in Berlin I went to Frankfort-on-Main to take part in a festival of two concerts devoted to my music.

My last stage was at Copenhagen, where I was to conduct a concert at the invitation of the great daily, *Dagens Nyheder*. As the Royal Opera in Copenhagen had just staged *Petroushka*, with the choreography reconstructed by Michel Fokine himself, the theatrical management, availing themselves of my presence, asked me to conduct one of the performances. I did so with great pleasure, leaving next day for Paris.

A few days after my arrival I was grieved to learn of the loss of a friend to whom I was sincerely attached. This was Ernest Oeberg, director of *Les Editions Russes*, founded by M. and Mme Koussevitzky, which had published most of my works. I deeply deplored the loss of this generous man, who had always had at heart anything touching my interests. Fortunately for me, he was succeeded by his collaborator, Gabriel Paitchadzé, who still carries on the work and in whom I have found a devoted friend.

Under the influence of all these unexpected events, I returned to Nice to spend Christmas.

IX

At the opening of the New Year I received from Cocteau the first part of his final version of *Oedipus* in the Latin translation of Jean Daniélou. I had been impatiently awaiting it for months, as I was eager to start work. All my expectations from Cocteau were fully justified. I could not have wished for a more perfect text, or one that better suited my requirements.

The knowledge of Latin, which I had acquired at school, but neglected, alas! for many years, began to revive as I plunged into the libretto, and, with the help of the French version, I rapidly familiarized myself with it. As I had fully anticipated, the events and characters of the great tragedy came to life wonderfully in this language, and, thanks to it, assumed a statuesque plasticity and a stately bearing entirely in keeping with the majesty of the ancient legend.

What a joy it is to compose music to a language of convention, almost of ritual, the very nature of which imposes a lofty dignity! One no longer feels dominated by the phrase, the literal meaning of the words. Cast in an immutable mold which adequately expresses their value, they do not require any further commentary. The text thus becomes purely phonetic material for the composer. He can dissect it at will and concentrate all his attention on its primary constituent element – that is to say, on the syllable. Was not this method of treating the text that of the old masters of austere style? This, too, has for centuries been the Church's attitude towards music, and has prevented it from falling into sentimentalism, and consequently into individualism.

To my great regret, I soon had to interrupt my work in

order to make another concert tour. I went to Amsterdam, where, for the first time, I tackled the *Sacre du Printemps*; thence to Rotterdam and Haarlem, and a little later to Budapest, Vienna, and Zagreb. On my way back to Nice I stopped at Milan to see Toscanini, who was to conduct *Le Rossignol* and *Petroushka*, which the Scala had decided to produce that spring. While in Vienna, I had read in the newspapers that the score of *Le Rossignol* had mysteriously disappeared from Toscanini's rehearsal room. It appears that during a short absence of Toscanini it had been taken from his music stand where, a few minutes earlier, he had been studying it. Search was immediately made, and it was at last found in the shop of an antique dealer, who had just purchased it from some person unknown. This incident had caused great excitement at the Scala, but it had already subsided by the time I reached Milan.

Toscanini received me in the most charming fashion. He called the choruses and asked me to accompany them on the piano in order to give them such instructions as I might think necessary. I was struck by the deep knowledge he had of the score in its smallest details, and by his meticulous study of every work which he undertook to conduct. This quality of his is universally recognized, but this was the first time that I had a chance of seeing it applied to one of my own compositions.

Everyone knows that Toscanini always conducts from memory. This is attributed to his shortsightedness. But in our days, when the number of showy conductors has so greatly increased, though in inverse ratio to their technical merits and their general culture, conducting an orchestra without the score had become the fashion, and is often a matter of mere display. There is, however, nothing mar-

129

velous about this apparent *tour de force* (unless the work is complicated by changes of tempo or rhythm, and in such cases it is not done, and for very good reasons); one risks little and with a modicum of assurance and coolness a conductor can easily get away with it. It does not really prove that he knows the orchestration of the score. But there can be no doubt on that point in the case of Toscanini. His memory is proverbial; there is not a detail that escapes him, as attendance at one of his rehearsals is enough to demonstrate.

I have never encountered in a conductor of such world repute such a degree of self-effacement, conscientiousness, and artistic honesty. What a pity it is that his inexhaustible energy and his marvelous talents should almost always be wasted on such eternally repeated works that no general idea can be discerned in the composition of his programs, and that he should be so unexacting in the selection of his modern repertory! I do not, however, wish to be misunderstood. I am far from reproaching Toscanini for introducing, let us say, the works of Verdi into his concerts. On the contrary, I wish that he did so oftener, since he conducts them in so pure a tradition. By so doing he might freshen all those symphonic programs which are built on one pattern and are all becoming unbearably moldy. If I am told that I have chosen my example badly, because Verdi is the author of purely vocal music, I reply that the Wagnerian fragments which have been specially adapted for the concert platform and are forever being repeated are also taken from so-called vocal works, and are equally devoid of symphonic form in the proper sense of the term.

Rejoicing in the knowledge that my work was in the hands of so eminent a *maestro*, I returned to Nice, but only a month later I got a telegram from the Scala saying that Toscanini had fallen ill and asking me to conduct the performances myself. I consented, and went to Milan at the beginning of May and conducted a series of performances which included my opera, *Le Rossignol*, with the incomparable Laura Pasini, and *Petroushka*, staged in the best tradition by the ballet master, Romanov. I was astounded by the high standard and rigorous discipline of the Scala orchestra, with which a month later I enjoyed making fresh contact when, at the invitation of Count G. Cicogna, president of the Societa de Ente Concerti Orchestrali, I returned to Milan again to play my *Concerto*.

During the rest of the summer and the following autumn and winter, I hardly stirred from home, being entirely absorbed by my work on *Oedipus*. The more deeply I went into the matter the more I was confronted by the problem of style (*tenue*) in all its seriousness. I am not here using the word *style* in its narrow sense, but am giving it a larger significance, a much greater range. Just as Latin, no longer being a language in everyday use, imposed a certain style on me, so the language of the music itself imposed a certain convention which would be able to keep it within strict bounds and prevent it from overstepping them and wandering into byways, in accordance with those whims of the author which are often so perilous. I had subjected myself to this restraint when I selected a form of language bearing the tradition of ages, a language which may be called homologous. The need for restriction, for deliberately submitting to a style, has its source in the very depths of our nature, and is found not only in matters of art, but in every conscious manifestation of human activity. It is the need for order without which nothing can be achieved, and upon the dis-

131

appearance of which everything disintegrates. Now all order demands restraint. But one would be wrong to regard that as any impediment to liberty. On the contrary, the style, the restraint, contribute to its development, and only prevent liberty from degenerating into license. At the same time, in borrowing a form already established and consecrated, the creative artist is not in the least restricting the manifestation of his personality. On the contrary, it is more detached, and stands out better when it moves within the definite limits of a convention. This it was that induced me to use the anodyne and impersonal formulas of a remote period and to apply them largely in my opera-oratorio, *Oedipus*, to the austere and solemn character to which they specially lent themselves.

I finished the score on March 14, 1927. As I have already said, we had decided with Cocteau that it should be heard in Paris for the first time, among Diaghileff's productions on the occasion of the twentieth anniversary of his theatrical activity, which occurred that spring. We, his friends, wished to commemorate the rare event in the annals of the theatre of an undertaking of a purely artistic nature, without the least hope of material gain, which had been able to continue for so many years and to survive so many trials including the World War, and had, moreover, continued solely owing to the indomitable energy, the persistent tenacity, of one man passionately devoted to his work. We wanted to give him a surprise, and were able to keep our secret to the last moment, which would have been impossible in the case of a ballet, for which Diaghileff's participation would have been necessary from the first. As we were too short both of time and funds to present *Oedipus Rex* in a stage setting, it was decided to give it in concert form. And even that entailed so large an outlay for soloists, choruses, and orchestra that we could never have met it if Princess Edmond de Polignac had not once more come to our assistance.

The first audition of *Oedipus* took place at the Théatre Sarah Bernhardt on May 30, and was followed by two more under my direction. Once again I had to suffer from the conditions under which my work was presented: an oratorio sandwiched between two ballets! An audience which had come to applaud ballet was naturally disconcerted by such a contrast, and was unable to concentrate on something purely auditive. That is why the later performances of *Oedipus* as an opera under Klemperer in Berlin, and then as a concert under my direction in Dresden and London and in the Salle Pleyel, Paris, gave me far greater satisfaction.

In June I spent a fortnight in London, where, besides conducting *Oedipus* for the British Broadcasting Corporation, I conducted a gala performance of my ballets given by Diaghileff in my honor, and which ex-King Alfonso, always faithful to the Russian Ballet, honored by his presence.

While in London I had an opportunity of hearing a very beautiful concert of the works of Manuel de Falla. With a decision and crispness meriting high praise, he conducted his remarkable *El Retablo de Maese Pedro*, in which he had the valuable assistance of Mme Vera Janacopoulos. I also greatly enjoyed hearing his concerto for harpsichord or piano, which he himself played on the latter instrument. In my opinion these two works give proof of incontestable progress in the development of his great talent. He has, in them, deliberately emancipated himself from the folklorist influence under which he was in danger of stultifying himself.

About this time I was asked by the Congressional Library in Washington to compose a ballet for a festival of contemporary music which was to include the production of several works specially written for the occasion. The generous American patron, Mrs. Elizabeth Sprague Coolidge, had undertaken to defray the expense of these artistic productions. I had a free hand as to subject and was limited only as to length, which was not to exceed half an hour by reason of the number of musicians to be heard in the available time. This proposal suited me admirably, for, as I was more or less free just then it enabled me to carry out an idea which had long tempted me, to compose a ballet founded on moments or episodes in Greek mythology plastically interpreted by dancing of the so-called classical school.

I chose as the theme Apollo Musagetes – that is Apollo as the master of the Muses, inspiring each of them with her own art. I reduced their number to three, selecting from among them Calliope, Polyhymnia, and Terpsichore as being the most characteristic representatives of choreographic art. Calliope, receiving the stylus and tablets from Apollo, personifies poetry and its rhythm; Polyhymnia, finger on lips, represents mime. As Cassiodorus tells us: "Those speaking fingers, that eloquent silence, those narratives in gesture, are said to have been invented by the Muse Polyhymnia, wishing to prove that man could express his will without recourse to words." Finally, Terpsichore, combining in herself both the rhythm of poetry and the eloquence of gesture, reveals dancing to the world, and thus among the Muses takes the place of honor beside the Musagetes.

After a series of allegorical dances, which were to be treated in the traditional classical style of ballet (*Pas d'action, Pas de deux, Variations, Coda*), Apollo, in an apotheosis, leads the Muses, with Terpsichore at their head, to Parnassus, where they were to live ever afterwards. I prefaced this allegory with a prologue representing the birth of Apollo. According to the legend, "Leto was with child, and, feeling the moment of birth at hand, threw her arms about a palm tree and knelt on the tender green turf, and the earth smiled beneath her, and the child sprang forth to the light. . . . Goddesses washed him with limpid water, gave him for swaddling clothes a white veil of fine tissue, and bound it with a golden girdle."

When, in my admiration for the beauty of line in classical dancing, I dreamed of a ballet of this kind, I had specially in my thoughts what is known as the "white ballet," in which to my mind the very essence of this art reveals itself in all its purity. I found that the absence of many-colored effects and of all superfluities produced a wonderful freshness. This inspired me to write music of an analogous character. It seemed to me that diatonic composition was the most appropriate for this purpose, and the austerity of its style determined what my instrumental ensemble must be. I at once set aside the ordinary orchestra because of its heterogeneity, with its groups of string, wood, brass, and percussion instruments. I also discarded ensembles of wood and brass, the effects of which have really been too much exploited of late, and I chose strings.

The orchestral use of strings has for some time suffered a sad falling off. Sometimes they are destined to support dynamic effects, sometimes reduced to the role of simple "colorists." I plead guilty myself in this respect. The original purpose of strings was determined in the country of their origin – Italy – and was first and foremost the cultivation of *canto*, of melody; but this, for good reasons, has been abandoned. There was a marked and warrantable reaction in the second half of the nineteenth century against a decay of melodic art which was congealing the language of music into hackneyed formulas while simultaneously neglecting many of the other elements of music. But, as so often happens, the swing of the pendulum was too violent. The taste for melody *per se* having been lost, it was no longer cultivated for its own sake, and there was therefore no criterion by which its value could be assessed. It seemed to me that it was not only timely but urgent to turn once more to the cultivation of this element from a purely musical point of view. That is why I was so much attracted by the idea of writing music in which everything should revolve about the melodic principle. And then the pleasure of immersing oneself again in the multisonorous euphony of strings and making it penetrate even the furthest fibers of the polyphonic web! And how could the unadorned design of the classical dance be better expressed than by the flow of melody as it expands in the sustained psalmody of strings?

I began the composition of *Apollo* in July. I was completely absorbed by the work, and, not wishing to be distracted, postponed till later all consideration of plans for the concerts which were to be given in the autumn. I did, however, accept the invitation of my friends the Lyons' – father and sons – directors of the Pleyel concern, to take part with Ravel in the opening of their large new concert hall in Paris. At this ceremony, attended by the highest Government officials of Paris, I conducted my *Suite de l'Oiseau de Feu*, and Ravel conducted his *Valse*. It was about this time that the Pleyel firm left the Rue Rochechouart, where it had been domiciled for nearly a century, and moved into new premises in the Faubourg St. Honoré, in which they gave me a studio. Meanwhile, all the rolls of my works made for their mechanical piano had been sold by Pleyel to the Duo Art

(Aeolian) Company, which signed a new contract with me that necessitated frequent journeys to London.

At the beginning of 1928 I finished composing the music of *Apollo*. All that now remained was the final orchestration of the score, and, as this did not occupy my whole time, I was able to give some of it to my tours and concerts. From among these I select for mention two at the Salle Pleyel, *Le Sacre du Printemps* being included in both programs. These concerts were important for me because it was the first time that Paris heard the *Sacre* under my direction. It is not for me to appraise my own performance, but I may say that, thanks to the experience I had gained with all kinds of orchestras on my numerous concert tours, I had reached a point at which I could obtain exactly what I wanted as I wanted it.

With regard to the *Sacre*, which I was tackling for the first time, I was particularly anxious in some of the parts (Glorification of the Elect, Evocation of Ancestors, Dance of Consecration) to give the bars their true metric value, and to have them played exactly as they were written. I lay stress on this point, which may seem to the reader to be a purely professional detail. But with a few exceptions, such as Monteux and Ansermet, for example, most conductors are inclined to cope with the metric difficulties of these passages in such cavalier fashion as to distort alike my music and my intentions. This is what happens: fearing to make a mistake in a sequence of bars of varying values, some conductors do not hesitate to ease their task by treating them as of equal length. By such methods the strong and weak *tempi* are obviously displaced, and it is left to the musicians to perform the onerous task of readjusting the accents in the new bars as improvised by the conductors, a task so difficult that even if there is no catastrophe the listener expects one at any moment, and is immersed in an atmosphere of intolerable strain.

There are other conductors who do not even try to solve the problem confronting them, and simply transcribe such music into undecipherable nonsense, which they try to conceal under violent gesticulations.

In listening to all these "artistic interpretations," one begins to feel profound respect for the honest skill of the artisan, and it is not without bitterness that I am compelled to say how seldom one finds artists who have it and use it, the rest disdaining it as something hierarchically inferior.

At the end of February I went to Berlin for the first performance of my *Oedipus*, which was being produced at the Staatsoper under Klemperer. It was what the Germans call an *Urauffuehrung*, that is to say, "world-first performance," for it was then, in Berlin, that it was given for the first time as an opera. The execution of *Oedipus*, which was followed by *Petroushka* and *Mavra*, was of the highest order. Musical life was at that time in full swing in Germany. In contrast with the pre-war custodians of old dogmas, a fresh public joyfully and gratefully accepted the new manifestations of contemporary art. Germany was definitely becoming the center of the musical movement, and spared no effort to make it succeed. In this connection I should like to mention the enlightened activity in the realm of music of such organizations as the *Rundfunk* (Radio) in Berlin and that of Frankfort-on-Main, and to note particularly the sustained efforts of the latter's admirable conductor, Rosbaud, who, by his energy, his taste, his experience, and devotion, succeeded very quickly in bringing that organization to a very high artistic pitch. My visits to Germany were then very frequent, and I always went there with the same pleasure.

After conducting two concerts at Barcelona, where I gave the *Sacre*, which up to then had not been heard there, I went to Rome to conduct my *Rossignol* at the Royal Opera, into which the old Costanzi Theatre had just been transformed. The management had at first intended to produce *Oedipus* also. It had been produced at the Staatsoper in Vienna under the direction of Schalk just as he was going to Berlin. But the plan had to be abandoned by reason of the overwhelming number of new productions for the opening of the Royal Opera.

I then went to Amsterdam to conduct *Oedipus* at the Concertgebouw, which was celebrating its fortieth anniversary by a series of sumptuous musical productions. The fine Concertgebouw orchestra, always at the same high level, the magnificent male choruses from the Royal Apollo Society, soloists of the first rank – among them Mme Hélène Sadoven as Jocasta, Louis van Tulder as Oedipus, and Paul Huf, an excellent reader – and the way in which my work was received by the public, have left a particularly precious memory that I recall with much enjoyment.

Soon afterwards I conducted *Oedipus* in London for the British Broadcasting Corporation. That institution, with which I had already worked for some years and with which I continue to be on the best of terms, merits special attention. A few well informed and cultured men – among them my friend of long standing, Edward Clark – have been able to form within this huge eclectic organization a small group which, with praiseworthy energy, pursues the propaganda of contemporary music, upholding its cause with invincible tenacity. The B.B.C. has succeeded in forming a fine orchestra, which certainly rivals the best in the world.

I should like here to say a few words about English musicians. The fact that England has not for a long time produced any great creators of music has given rise to an erroneous opinion concerning the musical gifts and aptitudes of the English in general. It is alleged that they are not musical; but this is contrary to my experience. I have nothing but praise for their ability, precision, and honest, conscientious work, as shown in all my dealings with them, and I have always been struck by the sincere and spontaneous enthusiasm which characterizes them in spite of inept prejudice to the contrary prevalent in other countries. I am not speaking merely of orchestral artists, but of choruses and solo singers, all alike devoted to their work. It is therefore not astonishing that I should always have been more than satisfied with their rendering of my works, and was so now with *Oedipus*, in which these qualities were fully displayed.

I seize this opportunity of paying a warm tribute to that veteran English conductor, Sir Henry Wood, a musician of the first rank, whose great gifts I had an opportunity of appreciating quite recently – in the autumn of 1934 – at a concert in which I conducted *Perséphone* and he most perfectly *L'Oiseau de Feu* and *Feu d'Artifice*, and accompanied me with so sure a hand when I played my *Capriccio*.

On my return to Paris I played my *Concerto* on May 19 under the excellent direction of Bruno Walter, who, thanks to his exceptional ability, made my task very pleasant, and I was quite free from anxiety over the rhythmically dangerous passages which are a stumbling block to so many conductors.

Some days later I conducted *Oedipus* at the Salle Pleyel, and this time, on the concert platform and before an audience attracted solely by the music, it produced a very different effect from that of its performance the year before in its setting among the productions of Russian Ballet.

Apropos of *Oedipus*, I remember hearing about that time that it had been given in Leningrad in the winter at a concert of the State Choral Academy under the direction of Klimoff, who had previously given *Les Noces*. In regard to the theatre in Russia I have been less fortunate. Under the old regime, nothing of mine was ever produced. The new regime at first seemed to be interested in my music. The state theatres produced my ballets – *Petroushka*, *L'Oiseau de Feu*, and *Pulcinella*. A clumsy attempt to stage *Renard* was a failure, and the piece was soon taken off. But after that, which was ten years ago, only *Petroushka* retained a place in the repertories, and it was rarely given at that. As for my other works, *Le Sacre*, *Les Noces*, *Le Soldat*, *Le Baiser de la Fée*, and my latest creation, *Perséphone*, have not yet seen the footlights in Russia. From this I conclude that a change of regime cannot change the truth of the old adage that no man is a prophet in his own country. One has only to recall the United States to show this. There, in the space of a few years, *Le Sacre*, *Les Noces*, and *Oedipus* have been successfully produced by Leopold Stokowski, under the auspices of the League of Composers; *Petroushka* and *Rossignol* at the Metropolitan Opera House, New York; and, still more recently, *Mavra*, in Philadelphia, under the direction of Alexander Smallens.

My ballet, *Apollo Musagetes*, was given in Washington for the first time on April 27, with Adolphe Bolm's choreography. As I was not there I cannot say anything about it. What interested me far more was its first performance in Paris at Diaghileff's theatre, inasmuch as I was myself to conduct the music. My orchestra was so small that I was able without difficulty to have four rehearsals. This gave me a chance to make a close study of the score with the musicians recruited from the great symphonic orchestras of Paris, whom I knew well, as I had frequently worked with them.

As I have already mentioned, *Apollo* was composed for string orchestra. My music demanded six groups instead of the quartet, as it is usually called, but, to be more exact, "quintet," of the ordinary orchestra, which is composed of first and second violins, violas, violoncellos, and double bass. I therefore added to the regular ensemble a sixth group, which was to be of second violoncellos. I thus formed an instrumental sextet, each group of which had a strictly defined part. This required the establishment of a well-proportioned gradation in the matter of the number of instruments for each group.

The importance of these proportions for the clarity and plasticity of the musical line was very clearly shown at a rehearsal of *Apollo* conducted by Klemperer in Berlin. From the very first pages I was struck by both the confusion of sound and the excessive resonance. Far from standing out in the ensemble, the various parts merged in it to such an extent that everything seemed drowned in an indistinct buzzing. And this happened notwithstanding the fact that the conductor knew the score perfectly, and scrupulously observed my movements and nuances. It was simply a matter of the proportions of which I have just been speaking, and which had not been foreseen. I drew Klemperer's attention to it immediately, and the necessary adjustments were made. His ensemble had consisted of sixteen first and fourteen second violins, ten violas, four first and four second violoncellos, and six double basses. The new arrangement was eight first and eight second violins, six violas, four first and four second violoncellos, and four double basses. The alteration immediately produced the desired effect. Everything became sharp and clear.

How often we composers are at the mercy of things of that sort, which seem so insignificant at first sight! How often it is just they that determine the impression made on the listener and decide the very success of the piece! Naturally the public does not understand, and judges the piece by the way in which it is presented. Composers may well envy the lot of painters, sculptors, and writers, who communicate directly with their public without having recourse to intermediaries.

On June 12 I conducted the first production of *Apollo Musagetes* at the Théatre Sarah Bernhardt in Paris. As a stage performance I got more satisfaction from this than from *Les Noces*, which was the latest thing that Diaghileff had had from me. Georges Balanchine, as ballet master, had arranged the dances exactly as I had wished – that is to say, in accordance with the classical school. From that point of view it was a complete success, and it was the first attempt to revive academic dancing in a work actually composed for the purpose. Balanchine, who had already given proof of great proficiency and imagination in his ballet productions, notably in the charming *Barabau* by Rieti, had designed for the choreography of Apollo groups, movements, and lines of great dignity and plastic elegance as inspired by the beauty of classical forms. As a thorough musician – he had studied at the St. Petersburg Conservatoire – he had had no difficulty in grasping the smallest details of my music, and his beautiful choreography clearly expressed my meaning. As for the dancers, they were beyond all praise. The graceful Nikitina with her purity of line alternating with the enchanting Danilova in the role of Terpsichore; Tchernichova and Doubrovska, those custodians of the best classical traditions; finally, Serge Lifar, then still quite young, conscientious, natural, spontaneous, and full of serious enthusiasm for his art – all these formed an unforgettable company. But my satisfaction was less complete in the matter of costume and *décor*, in which I did not see eye to eye with Diaghileff. As I have already said, I had pictured it to myself as danced in short white ballet skirts in a severely conventionalized theatrical landscape devoid of all fantastic embellishment such as would have been out of keeping with my primary conception. But Diaghileff, afraid of the extreme simplicity of my idea, and always on the lookout for something new, wished to enhance the spectacular side, and entrusted scenery and costumes to a provincial painter, little known to the Paris public – André Bauchant, who, in his remote village, indulged in a genre of painting somewhat in the style of the *douanier* Rousseau. What he produced was interesting, but, as I had expected, it in no way suited my ideas.

My work was very well received, and its success was greater than I had expected, seeing that the music of *Apollo* lacked those elements which evoked the enthusiasm of the public at a first hearing.

Directly after the Paris performance of *Apollo* I went to conduct it at its first London appearance. As always in England, where the Russian Ballet enjoys established and unwavering popularity, the piece was a great success, but it would be impossible to say in what degree this was due to music, author, dancers, choreography, subject, or scenery.

There was no rest for me that summer. I spent it at Echarvines, on the Lake of Annecy, where I had taken a room in a mason's cottage off the main road, and there I had installed a piano. I can never concentrate on my work if I am where I can be overheard, so that it was impossible for me to settle down with my piano in the boarding house in which I was staying with my family. I therefore chose this isolated place in the hope of finding peace and solitude, free from all importunate neighbors. I was cruelly deceived. The workman who had let the room to me occupied the rest of the house with his wife and child. He went out in the morning, and all was quiet till he returned at noon. The family then sat down to dinner. An acrid and nauseating smell of garlic and rancid oil came through the chinks of the partition which separated me from them, and made me feel sick. After an exchange of bitter words, the mason would lose his temper and begin to swear at his wife and child, terrifying them with his threats. The wife would start by answering, and then, bursting into sobs, would pick up the screaming infant and rush out, followed by her husband. This was repeated every day with hopeless regularity, so that the last hour of my morning's work was always filled with agonizing apprehension. Fortunately there was no need for me to return to the house in the afternoon, as I devoted that to work for which I did not require a piano.

One evening, when my sons and I were sitting quietly on the verandah of our boarding house, the silence of the night was suddenly shattered by piercing shrieks for help. I at once recognized the voice of the mason's wife, and my sons and I hurried across the little meadow which separated us from the house from which the cries were coming. But all was quiet; evidently our footsteps had been heard. Next day, at the request of the proprietor of our boarding house, the mayor of the village, who was aware of the goings-on of this charming family, expostulated with this desperate character over his cruelty to his wife. Whereupon the famous scene from Molière's *Médecin Malgré Lui* was repeated. Like Martine, the woman resolutely took her husband's part and declared that she had no reason to complain of him.

145

It was in that atmosphere that I worked at my *Baiser de la Fée*.

Just as I was finishing the music of Apollo at the end of the preceding year (1927), I received from Mme Ida Rubinstein a proposal to compose a ballet for her repertory. The painter Alexandre Benois, who did some work for her, submitted two plans, one of which seemed very likely to attract me. The idea was that I should compose something inspired by the music of Tchaikovsky. My well-known fondness for this composer, and, still more, the fact that November, the time fixed for the performance, would mark the thirty-fifth anniversary of his death, induced me to accept the offer. It would give me an opportunity of paying my heartfelt homage to Tchaikovsky's wonderful talent.

As I was free to choose both the subject and scenario of the ballet, I began to search for them, in view of the characteristic trend of Tchaikovsky's music, in the literature of the nineteenth century. With that aim, I turned to a great poet with a gentle, sensitive soul whose imaginative mind was wonderfully akin to that of the musician. I refer to Hans Christian Andersen, with whom in this respect Tchaikovsky had so much in common. To recall *La Belle au Bois Dormant*, *Casse Noisette*, *Le Lac des Cygnes*, *Pique Dame*, and many pieces of his symphonic work is enough to show the extent of his fondness for the fantastic.

In turning over the pages of Andersen with which I was fairly familiar, I came across a story I had completely forgotten, which struck me as being the very thing for the idea that I wanted to express. It was the very beautiful story known to us as *The Ice Maiden*. I chose that as my theme, and worked out the story on the following lines. A fairy imprints her magic kiss on a child at birth and parts it from its mother. Twenty years later, when the youth has attained the very zenith of his good fortune, she repeats the fatal kiss and carries him off to live in supreme happiness with her ever afterwards. As my object was to commemorate the work of Tchaikovsky, this subject seemed to me to be particularly appropriate as an allegory, the muse having similarly branded Tchaikovsky with her fatal kiss, and the magic imprint has made itself felt in all the musical creations of this great artist.

Although I gave full liberty to painter and choreographer in the staging of my composition, my innermost desire was that it should be presented in classical form, after the manner of *Apollo*. I pictured all the fantastic roles as danced in white ballet skirts, and the rustic scenes as taking place in a Swiss landscape, with some of the performers dressed in the manner of early tourists and mingling with the friendly villagers in the good old theatrical tradition.

As the date of Mme Rubinstein's performances was not far off, I barely left home all that summer except for a concert at Scheveningen, for I had not too much time in which to execute so complicated a piece of work. As I hate being hurried, and was afraid of unforseen obstacles towards the finish, I seized every hour I could to go ahead with my composition, thus leaving as little as possible to the last moments. I much preferred tiring myself at the beginning to being hurried at the end.

The following incident indicates how loath I was to waste time. The day on which I went to Paris on my way back to Nice, I found, on waking up in the train, that we were not in the suburbs of Paris, but in some wholly unexpected spot. It turned out that on account of the great number of extras put on by the railway to cope with the congestion caused by the end of the holidays our train had been shunted to a siding at Nevers, and I discovered that we should be four hours late in reaching Paris. Far from a station and on an empty stomach – not even a scrap of bread was available – I was nevertheless unperturbed by this mishap, and turned it to profit by working in my compartment during those four hours.

To finish and orchestrate my music in the short time available was so heavy a task that I was unable to follow the work of Bronislava Nijinska, who was composing the choreography in Paris bit by bit as I sent the parts from Echarvines as completed. Owing to this, it was not until just before the first performance that I saw her work, and by that time all the principal scenes had been fixed. I found some of the scenes successful and worthy of Nijinska's talent. But there was, on the other hand, a good deal of which I could not approve, and which, had I been present at the moment of their composition, I should have tried to get altered. But it was now too late for any interference on my part, and I had, whether I liked it or not, to leave things as they were. It is hardly surprising in these circumstances that the choreography of *Le Baiser de la Fée* left me cold.

I was generously given four rehearsals with the admirable orchestra of the Opera. They were arduous, because at each of them I had to contend with the dreadful system of deputizing – so fatal to the music when at each rehearsal musicians, without any warning, send others to take their place. One has only to recall the amusing story so often repeated, which is attributed to various conductors. Exasperated by seeing new faces at the instrumentalists' music stands at every rehearsal, he draws their attention to it, and suggests that they should follow the example of the soloist who regularly attends every rehearsal. At that moment the soloist rises, thanks the conductor, and informs him that on the day of the concert he will, to his great regret, have to send a deputy.

I conducted this ballet twice at the Paris Opera, on November 27 and December 4, at Mme Rubinstein's performances. It was also given once at the Théâtre de la Monnaie at Brussels, and once at Monte Carlo. On both these last occasions it was admirably conducted; in Brussels by Corneil de Thoran, and at Monte Carlo by Gustave Cloez. A final performance was given at the Scala at Milan about the same time, and after that Mme Rubinstein removed it from her repertory. A few years later, Bronislava Nijinska produced it again at the Teatro Colon at Buenos Aires, where she had already given Les Noces, and where both these works had a great success. Nor was this an isolated incident. In the course of the last eight years most of my symphonic and stage compositions have frequently played at Buenos Aires, and, thanks to Ansermet's conducting, the public has been able to get a good idea of them.

As with my other ballets, I made an orchestral suite from the music of Le Baiser de la Fee, which can be played without much difficulty by reason of the restricted size of the orchestra required. I often conduct this suite myself, and I like doing so, all the more because in it I tried a style of writing and orchestration which was new to me, and was one by means of which the music could be appreciated at the first hearing.

At the beginning of the 1928–1929 season a new organization came into being, known as the Orchestre Symphonique de Paris, or O.S.P., created by Ansermet, who became its principal conductor. At its invitation, I conducted two concerts at the Théatre des Champs-Elysées with this new group, and it was a joy to work with these young musicians, who were so well disciplined and so full of goodwill, and who were forbidden to indulge the odious habit of deputizing, of which all conductors complain and from which I suffered so much at the rehearsals of *Le Baiser de la Fée*.

About this time I signed a contract for several years with the great Columbia Gramophone Company, for which I was exclusively to record my work both as pianist and conductor, year by year. This work greatly interested me, for here, far better than with piano rolls, I was able to express all my intentions with real exactitude.

Consequently these records, very successful from a technical point of view, have the importance of documents which can serve as guides to all executants of my music. Unfortunately, very few conductors avail themselves of them. Some do not even inquire whether such records exist. Doubtless their dignity prevents others from consulting them, especially since if once they knew the record they could not with a clear conscience conduct as they liked. Is it not amazing that in our times, when a sure means which is accessible to all, has been found of learning exactly how the author demands his work to be executed, there should still be those who will not take any notice of such means, but persist in inserting concoctions of their own vintage?

Unfortunately, therefore, the rendering recorded by the author fails to achieve its most important object – that of safeguarding his work by establishing the manner in which it ought to be played. This is all the more regrettable since it is not a question of a haphazard gramophone record of just any performance. Far from that, the very purpose of the work on these records is the elimination of all chance elements by selecting from among the different records those which are most successful. It is obvious that in even the very best records one may come across certain defects such as crackling, a rough surface, excessive or insufficient resonance. But these defects, which, for that matter, can be more or less corrected by the gramophone and the choice of the needle, do not in the least affect the essential thing, without which it would be impossible to form any idea of the composition — I refer to the pace of the movements and their relationship to one another.

When one thinks of the complexity of making such records, of all the difficulties it presents, of all the accidents to which it is exposed, the constant nervous strain caused by the knowledge that one is continuously at the mercy of some possible stroke of bad luck, some extraneous noise by reason of which it may all have to be done over again, how can one help being embittered by the thought that the fruit of so much labor will be so little used, even as a document, by the very persons who should be most interested?

One cannot even pretend that the easygoing fashion in which "interpreters" treat their contemporaries is because they feel that these contemporaries have not sufficient reputation to matter. The old masters, the classics, are subject to just the same treatment notwithstanding all their authority. It is enough to cite Beethoven and to take as an illustration his Eighth Symphony, which bears the composer's own precise metronomic directions. But are they heeded? There are as many different renderings as there are conductors! "Have you heard *my* Fifth, *my* Eighth?" — that is a phrase that has become quite usual in the mouths of these gentlemen, and their mentality could not be better exemplified.

But, no matter how disappointing the work is when regarded from this point of view, I do not for a moment regret the time and effort spent on it. It gives me the satisfaction of knowing that everyone who listens to my records hears my music free from any distortion of my thought, at least in its essential elements. Moreover, the work did a good deal to develop my technique as a conductor. The frequent repetition of a fragment or even of an entire piece, the sustained effort to allow not the slightest detail to escape attention, as may happen for lack of time at any ordinary rehearsal, the necessity of observing absolute precision of movement as strictly determined by the timing – all this is a hard school in which a musician obtains very valuable training and learns much that is extremely useful.

In the domain of music the importance and influence of its dissemination by mechanical means, such as the record and the radio – those redoubtable triumphs of modern science which will probably undergo still further development – make them worthy of the closest investigation. The facilities that they offer to composers and executants alike for reaching great numbers of listeners, and the opportunities that they give to those listeners of acquainting themselves with works they have not heard, are obviously indisputable advantages. But one must not overlook the fact that such advantages are attended by serious danger. In John Sebastian Bach's day it was necessary for him to walk ten miles to a neighboring town to hear Buxtehude play his works. Today anyone, living no matter where, has only to turn a knob or put on a record to hear what he likes. Indeed, it is in just this incredible facility, this lack of necessity for any effort, that the evil of this so-called progress lies. For in music, more than in any other branch of art, understanding is given only to those who make an active effort. Passive receptivity is not

enough. To listen to certain combinations of sound and auto-
matically become accustomed to them does not necessarily
imply that they have been heard and understood. For one can
listen without hearing, just as one can look without seeing.
The absence of active effort and the liking acquired for this
facility make for laziness. The radio has got rid of the necessity which existed in Bach's day for getting out of one's arm-
chair. Nor are listeners any longer impelled to play themselves, or to spend time on learning an instrument in order to
acquire a knowledge of musical literature. The wireless and
the gramophone do all that. And thus the active faculties of
listeners, without which one cannot assimilate music, gradually become atrophied from lack of use. This creeping
paralysis entails very serious consequences. Oversaturated
with sounds, *blasé* even before combinations of the utmost
variety, listeners fall into a kind of torpor which deprives
them of all power of discrimination and makes them indifferent to the quality of the pieces presented. It is more than
likely that such irrational overfeeding will make them lose
all appetite and relish for music. There will, of course, always
be exceptions, individuals who will know how to select from
the mass those things that appeal to them. But for the majority of listeners there is every reason to fear that, far from
developing a love and understanding of music, the modern
methods of dissemination will have a diametrically opposite
effect – that is to say, the production of indifference, inability
to understand, to appreciate, or to undergo any worthy reaction.

In addition, there is the musical deception arising from
the substitution for the actual playing of a reproduction,
whether on record or film or by wireless transmission from a
distance. It is the same difference as that between the *ersatz*

and the authentic. The danger lies in the very fact that there is always a far greater consumption of the *ersatz*, which, it must be remembered, is far from being identical with its model. The continuous habit of listening to changed and sometimes distorted, timbres spoils the ear, so that it gradually loses all capacity for enjoying natural musical sounds.

All these considerations may seem unexpected in coming from one who has worked so much, and is still working, in this field. I think that I have sufficiently stressed the instructional value that I unreservedly ascribe to this means of musical reproduction; but that does not prevent me from seeing its negative sides, and I anxiously ask myself whether they are sufficiently outweighed by the positive advantages to enable one to face them with impunity.

X

I have now brought my chronicle up to the year 1929, a year overshadowed by a great and grievous event – the passing of Diaghileff. He died on August 19, but his loss moved me so profoundly that it dwarfs in my memory all the other events of that year. I shall, therefore, somewhat anticipate the chronology of my narrative in order to speak here of my late friend.

At the beginning of my career he was the first to single me out for encouragement, and he gave me real and valuable assistance. Not only did he like my music and believe in my development, but he did his utmost to make the public appreciate me. He was genuinely attracted by what I was then writing, and it gave him real pleasure to produce my work, and, indeed, to force it on the more rebellious of my listeners, as for example, in the case of the *Sacre du Printemps*. These feelings of his, and the zeal which characterized them, naturally evoked in me a reciprocal sense of gratitude, deep attachment, and admiration for his sensitive comprehension, his ardent enthusiasm, and the indomitable fire with which he put things into practice.

Our friendship, which lasted for almost twenty years, was, alas! marked from time to time by conflicts which, as I have already said, were due to his extreme jealousy. It is obvious that my relations with Diaghileff could not but undergo a certain change in the later years in view of the broadening of the field of my personal and independent activities, and of the fact that my collaboration with the Russian Ballet had lost the continuity it had earlier enjoyed. There was less affinity than before in our ideas and opinions, which, as time went on, frequently developed in divergent directions. "Modernism" at any price, cloaking a fear of not being in the vanguard; the search for something sensational; uncertainty as to what line to take – these things wrapped Diaghileff in a morbid atmosphere of painful gropings. All this prevented me from being in sympathy with everything he did, and this made us less frank in our relations with each other. Rather than upset him, I evaded these questions, especially as my arguments would have served no useful purpose. It is true that with age and ill health his self-assurance had decreased, but not his temperament or his habitual obstinacy, and he would certainly have persisted in a heated defense of things which I felt sure that he was not certain about in his innermost being.

My last contact with Diaghileff was in connection with

Renard, which he was re-creating for his spring season at the Théatre Sarah Bernhardt. Without entering here into a discussion of the new setting, I must say that I missed the first version created by Nijinska in 1922, of which I have already spoken.

After that season in Paris I saw him only once – casually, and at a distance on the platform of the Gare du Nord, where we were both taking the train for London. Six weeks later the news of his death reached me at Echarvines, where I was spending the summer as I had done the year before. I had been out with my sons to see Prokoviev, who was living in the neighborhood. On returning late, we were met by my wife, who had sat up to give us the sad news which had been telegraphed from Venice.

I was not entirely unprepared for his death. I knew that he had diabetes, though I did not know that it was so serious as to be dangerous, especially as at his age his robust constitution should have enabled him to combat the disease for some years. His physical condition had not, therefore, caused me any alarm. But, of late, in watching the usual activities of his everyday life, I had formed the impression that his moral forces were rapidly disintegrating, and I was haunted by the thought that he had reached the limit of his life. That is why his death, though it caused me acute grief as our final parting, did not greatly surprise me.

At the moment I naturally did not give much thought to an estimate of the influence of Diaghileff's activity, indeed of his very life, in the world of art. I gave myself up to my grief, mourning a friend, a brother, whom I should never see again.

This separation gave rise to many feelings, many memories, which were dear to me. It is only today, with the passing of the years, that one begins to realize everywhere and in everything what a terrible void was created by the disappearance of this colossal figure, whose greatness can only be measured fully by the fact that it is impossible to replace him. The truth of the matter is that everything that is original is irreplaceable. I recall this fine phrase of the painter Constantine Korovine: "I thank you," he said one day to Diaghileff, "I thank you for being alive."

I devoted most of 1929 to the composition of my *Capriccio*, which I had begun the Christmas before. As so often happened with me, this work was several times interrupted by unavoidable journeys. In February I went to conduct *Oedipus* at a concert in the Dresden Opera House, where I was particularly impressed by the incomparable finish of the Dresdner Lehrergesangsverein choirs. *Oedipus* was the sole item on the program, and was given twice on the same day – at a public general rehearsal at noon, and at the concert itself in the evening.

A little later La Société Philharmonique de Paris asked me to conduct a concert of my chamber music. It took place at the Salle Pleyel on March 5. The program included *L'Histoire d'un Soldat* and the *Octuor*, and I myself played my *Sonate* and my *Sérénade* for the piano. I take this opportunity of expressing my appreciation of that admirable group of Paris soloists who have for many years lent their talent and their wonderful enthusiasm to enhance the value of my work, whether in concerts, in the theatre, or in the fatiguing process of making records. I want particularly to mention Darieu and Merckel (violins), Boussagol (double bass), Moyse (flute), Gaudeau (clarinet), Dherin and Grandmaison (bassoons), Vignal and Foveau (trumpets), Delbos and Tudesque (trombones), and Morel (percussion).

My visits to London stand out among the pleasant memories of my journeys that year. London is so delightful at the beginning of the summer, with its green lawns, the beautiful trees in the parks, the river on its outskirts gay with numberless boats, and everywhere the frank good humor of healthy athletic youth. In such an atmosphere work is easy, and I much enjoyed playing my *Concerto* with that brilliant English musician, Eugène Goossens, as conductor, and myself conducting *Apollo* and – for the first time in England – *Le Baiser de la Fée* for the B.B.C.

The enjoyment of my few days in London was enhanced by the presence of Willy Strecker, one of the owners of the publishing firm of Schott Söhne at Mainz, a clever, cultured man with whom, apart from business relations, I am on the friendliest terms, as indeed I am with all his charming family, who always give me the kindest welcome when I go to Wiesbaden, where they live.

At that time Diaghileff's Russian Ballet was taking part in the *Festspiele* season in Berlin. Their performances were being given at the two state theatres – at the Opera, Unter den Linden, and at the Charlottenburg Opera. *Le Sacre du Printemps* and *Apollo* were among the works which had their first stage performance there. A few days earlier Klemperer had given *Apollo* a first hearing at a concert of my music, in which I played my *Concerto*. I was prevented from seeing the Diaghileff performances, as I was urgently wanted in Paris to make some gramophone records, and I did not regret it. I knew that the ballets were to come at the end of the *Festspiele*, when the orchestras of the two theatres would be worn out by their heavy work throughout the festival season. Besides, as always happened when the Ballet was on tour, all that the theatres or impresarios cared about was the scenic effects, troubling very little about the musical aspect, though trying to find composers whose names would attract the public. In this case the same conditions prevailed, so that, notwithstanding all the efforts of a conductor like Ansermet, I expect that my absence saved me from a somewhat painful impression.

I worked at my *Capriccio* all summer and finished it at the end of September. I played it for the first time on December 6 at a Paris Symphony Orchestra concert, Ansermet conducting. I had so often been asked in the course of the last few years to play my *Concerto* (this I had already done no fewer than forty times) that I thought that it was time to give the public another work for piano and orchestra. That is why I wrote another concerto, which I called *Capriccio*, that name seeming to indicate best the character of the music. I had in mind the definition of a *capriccio* given by Praetorius, the celebrated musical authority of the eighteenth century. He regarded it as a synonym of the *fantasia*, which was a free form made up of *fugato* instrumental passages. This form enabled me to develop my music by the juxtaposition of episodes of various kinds which follow one another and by their very nature give the piece that aspect of caprice from which it takes its name.

There is little wonder that, while working at my *Capriccio*, I should find my thoughts dominated by that prince of music, Carl Maria von Weber, whose genius admirably lent itself to this manner. Alas! no one thought of calling him a prince in his lifetime! I cannot refrain from quoting (authentically) the startling opinion that the celebrated Viennese dramatic poet, Franz Grillparzer, had of *Euryanthe* and its composer; I found it in a striking anthology of classical criticism published by Schott. It runs as follows: "What I had

159

feared on the appearance of *Freischütz* seems now to be confirmed. Weber certainly has a poetical mind, but he is no musician. Not a trace of melody, not merely of pleasing melody but of any sort of melody. . . . Tatters of ideas held together solely by the text, without any inherent musical sequence. There is no invention; even the way in which the libretto is handled is devoid of originality. A total lack of arrangement and color. . . . This music is horrible. This inversion of euphony, this violation of beauty, would in ancient Greece have been punished by the state with penal sanctions. Such music is contrary to police regulations. It would give birth to monstrosities if it managed to get about."

It is quite certain that no one would dream nowadays of sharing Grillparzer's indignation. Far from that; those who consider themselves advanced, if they know Weber, and still more if they do not know him, make a merit of treating him with contempt as a musician who is too easy, out of date, and at the best can appeal only to old fogies. Such an attitude might perhaps be understandable on the part of those who are musically illiterate, and whose self-assurance is too often equaled only by their incompetence. But what can be said for professional musicians when they are capable of expressing such opinions as, for example, those I have heard from Scriabine? It is true that he was not speaking of Weber, but of Schubert, but that does not alter the case. One day when Scriabine with his usual emphasis was pouring out ideological verbosities concerning the sublimity of art and its great pontiffs, I, on my side, began to praise the grace and elegance of Schubert's waltzes, which I was replaying at the time with real pleasure. With an ironical smile of commiseration he said: "Schubert? But look here, that is only fit to be strummed on the piano by little girls!"

The Boston Symphony Orchestra decided that winter to celebrate its fiftieth anniversary, which would fall in 1930, by a series of festivals. This famous organization wished to give them a special interest by presenting symphonic works specially written for the occasion by contemporary composers. Koussevitzky, who has been at the head of this admirable orchestra for years, asked me to cooperate by composing a symphony for them.

The idea of writing a symphonic work of some length had been present in my mind for a long time, and I therefore gladly accepted a proposal so thoroughly in accord with my wishes. I had a free hand alike as to the form of the work and as to the means of execution I might think necessary. I was tied only by the date for the delivery of the score, but that allowed me ample time.

Symphonic form as bequeathed to us by the nineteenth century held little attraction for me, inasmuch as it had flourished in a period the language and ideas of which were all the more foreign to us because it was the period from which we emerged. As in the case of my *Sonate*, I wanted to create an organic whole without conforming to the various models adopted by custom, but still retaining the periodic order by which the symphony is distinguished from the suite, the latter being simply a succession of pieces varying in character.

I also had under consideration the sound material with which to build my edifice. My idea was that my symphony should be a work with great contrapuntal development, and for that it was necessary to increase the media at my disposal. I finally decided on a choral and instrumental ensemble in which the two elements should be on an equal footing, neither of them outweighing the other. In this instance my point of view as to the mutual relationship of the vocal and instrumental sections coincided with that of the masters of contrapuntal music, who also treated them as equals, and neither reduced the role of the choruses to that of homophonous chant nor the function of the instrumental ensemble to that of an accompaniment.

I sought for my words, since they were to be sung, among those which had been written for singing. And quite naturally my first idea was to have recourse to the Psalms. Soon after the first performance of my symphony, a criticism was forwarded to me in which its author asked: "Has the composer attempted to be Hebrew in his music – Hebrew in spirit, after the manner of Ernest Bloch, but without too much that is reminiscent of the synagogue?"

This gentleman does not seem to know that after two thousand years the Psalms are not necessarily associated with the synagogue, but are the main foundation of the prayers, orisons, and chants of the Church. But, apart from his real or pretended ignorance, does not the ridiculous question he asks reveal only too clearly a mentality that one encounters more and more frequently today? Apparently people have lost all capacity to treat the Holy Scriptures otherwise than from the point of view of ethnography, history, or picturesqueness. That anyone should take his inspiration from the Psalms without giving a thought to these side issues appears to be incredible to them, and so they demand explanations. Yet it seems quite natural to them that a piece of jazz should be called *Alleluia*. All these misunderstandings arise from the fact that people will always insist upon looking in music for something that is not there. The main thing for them is to know what the piece expresses, and what the author had in mind when he composed it. They never seem to understand that music has an entity of its own apart from anything that it may suggest to them. In other words, music interests them in so far as it touches on elements outside it while evoking sensations with which they are familiar.

Most people like music because it gives them certain emotions, such as joy, grief, sadness, an image of nature, a subject for daydreams, or – still better – oblivion from "everyday life." They want a drug – "dope." It matters little whether this way of thinking of music is expressed directly or is wrapped up in a veil of artificial circumlocutions. Music would not be worth much if it were reduced to such an end. When people have learned to love music for itself, when they listen with other ears, their enjoyment will be of a far higher and more potent order, and they will be able to judge it on a higher plane and realize its intrinsic value. Obviously such an attitude presupposes a certain degree of musical development and intellectual culture, but that is not very difficult of attainment. Unfortunately, the teaching of music, with a few exceptions, is bad from the beginning. One has only to think of all the sentimental twaddle so often talked about Chopin, Beethoven, and even about Bach – and that in schools for the training of professional musicians! Those tedious commentaries on the side issues of music not only do not facilitate its understanding, but, on the contrary, are a serious obstacle which prevents the understanding of its essence and substance.

All these considerations were evoked by my *Symphonie des Psaumes* because, both by the public and the press, the attitude I have just described was specially manifested in regard to that work. Notwithstanding the interest aroused by the composition, I noticed a certain perplexity caused, not by the music as such, but by the inability of listeners to under-

163

stand the reason which had led me to compose a symphony in a spirit which found no echo in their mentality.

As always of late years, my work on the *Symphonie des Psaumes*, begun about the New Year, suffered many interruptions by reason of the numerous European concerts in which I took part either as pianist or conductor. The *Capriccio*, my latest composition, was already in demand in various towns. I had to play it at Berlin, Leipzig, Bucharest, Prague, and Winterthur. Moreover, I had to conduct concerts at Dusseldorf, Brussels, and Amsterdam. But by the beginning of the summer I was at last able to devote all my time to the symphony, of which, so far, I had finished only one part. I had to write the whole of the other two parts, and did so, partly at Nice, partly at Charavines, where I spent the latter part of the summer on the shore of the little Lake Paladru. I put the final touches to the music on August 15, and was then able to concentrate quietly on the orchestration which I had begun at Nice.

My peregrinations began again in the autumn, and continued till December. I toured all central Europe, beginning with Switzerland (Basle, Zurich, Lausanne, Geneva), and ending with Brussels and Amsterdam. Besides that, and in addition to Berlin and Vienna, I visited Mainz, Wiesbaden, Bremen, Munich, Nuremberg, Frankfort-on-Main, and Mannheim, nearly always playing my *Capriccio* or conducting my works.

The first European audition of the *Symphonie des Psaumes* took place at the Palais des Beaux Arts of Brussels, under the direction of Ansermet. Koussevitzky gave it in Boston at the same time. The Brussels concert at which I played my *Capriccio*, which was repeated on the following day, has left a very pleasant memory. Many friends had come from Paris to hear my new work, and I was deeply touched by their sympathy and the warmth of the reception that the symphony received from the public. As was to be expected, the execution was perfect, and the admirable choruses of the Société Philharmonique once more lived up to the reputation for expert proficiency which they so justly enjoy in Belgium.

While at Mainz and Wiesbaden I frequently saw Willy Strecker. He talked to me a good deal about a young violinist, Samuel Dushkin, with whom he had become very friendly and whom I had never met. In the course of our conversations he asked me whether I should care to write something for the violin, adding that in Dushkin I should find a remarkable executant. I hesitated at first, because I am not a violinist, and I was afraid that my slight knowledge of that instrument would not be sufficient to enable me to solve the many problems which would necessarily arise in the course of a major work specially composed for it. But Willy Strecker allayed my doubts by assuring me that Dushkin would place himself entirely at my disposal in order to furnish any technical details I might require. Under such conditions the plan was very alluring, particularly as it would give me a chance of studying seriously the special technique of the violin. When he learned that I had in principle accepted Strecker's proposal, Dushkin came to Wiesbaden to make my acquaintance. I had not previously met him or heard him play. All I knew was that he had studied the violin and music in general in America, where, in his early childhood, he had been adopted by the American composer, Blair Fairchild, a man of great distinction, rare kindness, and a mind remarkable for its delicate sensibility.

From our first meeting I could see that Dushkin was all that Willy Strecker had said. Before knowing him I had been a little doubtful, in spite of the weight that I attached to the recommendations of a man of such finished culture as my friend Strecker. I was afraid of Dushkin as a virtuoso. I knew that for virtuosi there were temptations and dangers that they were not all capable of overcoming. In order to succeed they are obliged to seek immediate triumphs and to lend themselves to the wishes of the public, the great majority of whom demand sensational effects from the player. This preoccupation naturally influences their taste, their choice of music, and their manner of treating the piece selected. How many admirable compositions, for instance, are set aside because they do not offer the player any opportunity of shining with facile brilliancy! Unfortunately, they often cannot help themselves, fearing the competition of their rivals and, to be frank, the loss of their bread and butter.

Dushkin is certainly an exception in this respect among many of his fellow players, and I was very glad to find in him, besides his remarkable gifts as a born violinist, a musical culture, a delicate understanding, and – in the exercise of his profession – an abnegation that is very rare. His beautiful mastery of technique comes from the magnificent school of Leopold Auer, that marvelous teacher to whose instruction we owe nearly all the celebrated violinists of today. A Jew, like the great majority of leading violinists, Dushkin possesses all those innate gifts which make representatives of that race the unquestionable masters of the violin. The greatest names among these virtuosi have in fact a Jewish sound. Their owners should be proud of them and it is difficult to understand why most of them persist in prefixing Russian diminutives such as are generally used only among intimates. Instead of Alexander they call themselves Sacha; instead of Jacob or James, Yasha; instead of Michael, Misha. Being ignorant of the language and usages of Russia, foreigners can have no idea of how such lack of taste jars. It is as though one spoke of Julot Massenet or Popol Dukas!

I began the composition of the first part of my *Concerto pour Violon* early in 1931. I had devoted about a month to it when I was obliged to leave it for the time being, as I had to go to Paris and London. In Paris I took part in two concerts given by Ansermet. In the first, on February 20, I played my *Capriccio*, and on February 24 I conducted my *Symphonie des Psaumes* at its first Paris audition. On this occasion my work with the orchestra was particularly interesting to me because the Columbia firm had arranged with Ansermet that records should be made of the symphony at the Théatre des Champs-Elysées, during which I was to prepare for the concert. The performance could not fail to benefit by this, as the rehearsals had to be conducted with that exceptionally minute care which, as I have already pointed out, is demanded by all records.

It was at the Courtauld-Sargent Concerts, on March 3 and 4, that I played my *Capriccio* for the first time in London. These concerts bear the name of their founder, Mrs. Courtauld, who, animated by the best intentions, ably seconded by the conductor Sargent, had by her energy infused life into a musical undertaking which might well have become still more important under her influence. She was the patron of young artists and sincerely interested in new works, so that the programs of her concerts were frequently differentiated by their freshness from the routine and colorless programs which generally characterize the musical life of great centers, London included. Alas! patrons of her quality become more and more rare, and the premature death of this generous benefactor cannot be too deeply deplored. The organization survives her death, but no longer bears the special imprint given by the enthusiasm of its founder.

I was glad to return to Nice and be able to take up my *Concerto* again. The first part was completed at the end of March, and I began the other two. This took up all my time, and it was made particularly pleasant by the enthusiasm and understanding with which Dushkin followed my progress. I was not a complete novice in handling the violin. Apart from my pieces for the string quartet and numerous passages in *Pulcinella*, I had had occasion, particularly in the *Histoire d'un Soldat*, to tackle the technique of the violin as a solo instrument. But a concerto certainly offered a far vaster field of experience. To know the technical possibilities of an instrument without being able to play it is one thing; to have that technique in one's finger tips is quite another. I realized the difference, and before beginning the work I consulted Hindemith, who is a perfect violinist. I asked him whether the fact that I did not play the violin would make itself felt in my composition. Not only did he allay my doubts, but he went further and told me that it would be a very good thing, as it would make me avoid a routine technique, and would give rise to ideas which would not be suggested by the familiar movement of the fingers.

I had barely begun the composition of the last part of the *Concerto* when I had to see to our removal from Nice to Voreppe in Isère, where I had taken a small property for the summer. I had decided to leave Nice after having lived there for seven years, and at first thought of living in Paris, but the pure air of the Isère valley, the peacefulness of the country, a very beautiful garden, and a large, comfortable house induced us to settle there for good, and there we stayed for three years. There I finished my latest composition among half-unpacked trunks and boxes and the coming and going of removers, upholsterers, electricians, and plumbers. My faithful Dushkin, who was near Grenoble and not far from us, used to come to see me every day. He was assiduously studying his part so as to be ready in time, as the Berlin Rundfunk had secured the first audition of the *Concerto*, which was to be played under my direction on October 23.

After conducting concerts at Oslo, I went to Berlin. There my new work was very well received, as it was also in Frankfort-on-Main, London, Cologne, Hanover, and Paris, where Dushkin and I played in November and December. In an interval between concerts at Halle and Darmstadt, I spent about a fortnight at Wiesbaden, and so was able to hear the first performance of a new composition by Hindemith – his cantata *Das Unaufhörliche*, given at the centenary festival of the Mainz Liedertafel. This composition, large alike in size and substance and the varied character of its parts, offers an excellent opportunity for getting into touch with the author's individuality, and for admiring his rich talent and brilliant mastery. The appearance of Hindemith in the musical life of our day is very fortunate, for he stands out as a wholesome and illuminating principle amid so much obscurity.

Far from having exhausted my interest in the violin, my *Concerto*, on the contrary, impelled me to write yet another important work for that instrument. I had formerly had no great liking for a combination of piano and strings, but a deeper knowledge of the violin and close collaboration with a technician like Dushkin had revealed possibilities I longed to explore. Besides, it seemed desirable to open up a wider field for my music by means of chamber concerts, which are so much easier to arrange, as they do not require large orchestras of high quality, which are so costly and so rarely to be found except in big cities. This gave me the idea of writing a sort of sonata for violin and piano that I called *Duo Concertant* and which, together with transcriptions of a few of my other works, was to form the program of recitals that I proposed to give with Dushkin in Europe and America.

I began the *Duo Concertant* at the end of 1931 and finished it on the July 15 following. Its composition is closely connected in my mind with a book which had just appeared and which had greatly delighted me. It was the remarkable *Petrarch* of Charles Albert Cingria, an author of rare sagacity and deep originality. Our work had a great deal in common. The same subjects occupied our thoughts, and, although we were now living far apart and seldom saw each other, the close agreement between our views, our tastes, and our ideas, which I had noticed when we first met twenty years before, not only still existed, but seemed even to have grown with the passing of the years.

"Lyricism cannot exist without rules, and it is essential that they should be strict. Otherwise there is only a faculty for lyricism, and that exists everywhere. What does not exist everywhere is lyrical expression and composition. To achieve that, apprenticeship to a trade is necessary." These words of Cingria seemed to apply with the utmost appropriateness to the work I had in hand. My object was to create a lyrical composition, a work of musical versification, and I was more than ever experiencing the advantage of a rigorous discipline which gives a taste for the craft and the satisfaction of being able to apply it – and more particularly in work of a lyrical character. It would be appropriate to quote in this connection the words of one who is regarded above all as a lyrical composer. This is what Tchaikovsky says in one of his letters: "Since I began to compose I have made it my object to be, in my craft, what the most illustrious masters were in theirs;

that is to say, I wanted to be, like them, an artisan, just as a shoemaker is. . . . (They) composed their immortal works exactly as a shoemaker makes shoes; that is to say, day in, day out, and for the most part to order." How true that is! Did not Bach, Handel, Haydn, Mozart, Beethoven, to cite the best-known names, and even leaving the early Italians out of consideration, compose their works in that way?

The spirit and form of my *Duo Concertant* were determined by my love of the pastoral poets of antiquity and their scholarly art and technique. The theme that I had chosen developed through all the five movements of the piece which forms an integral whole, and, as it were, offers a musical parallel to the old pastoral poetry.

The work was interrupted only by a few concerts at Antwerp, Florence, and Milan. Its first performance was in Berlin on October 28, 1932, at the broadcasting station, where, under my direction, Dushkin also played my *Concerto pour Violon*. We then gave a series of recitals for piano and violin, the programs including the above mentioned transcriptions as well as the *Duo Concertant*. We played that winter at Danzig, Paris, Munich, London, and Winterthur, and in between I conducted and played at Königsberg, Hamburg, Ostrava, Paris, Budapest, Milan, Turin, and Rome. My visits to the Italian towns left a particularly pleasant impression. I am always delighted to go to Italy, a country for which I have the deepest admiration. And this admiration is increased by the marvelous regenerative effort which has manifested itself there for the last ten years, and is still manifesting itself in every direction. I had proof of this in my own domain when I conducted my works – among others, the *Symphonie des Psaumes* – with the orchestra of the Turin Radio, a new and distinguished organization.

At the beginning of 1933, Mme Ida Rubinstein had inquired whether I would consent to write the music for a poem by André Gide, which he had planned before the war and which Mme Rubinstein wished to stage. I agreed in principle, and at the end of January André Gide joined me at Wiesbaden, where I happened to be staying. He showed me his poem, which was taken from the superb Homeric hymn to Demeter. The author expressed his willingness to make any modification in the text required by the music and under such conditions an agreement was quickly reached. A few months later I received the first part of the poem and set to work on it.

With the exception of two melodies for some lines by Verlaine, this was my first experience of composing music for French words. I had always been afraid of the difficulties of French prosody. Although I had been living in France for twenty years, and had spoken the language from childhood, I had until now hesitated to use it in my music. I now decided to try my hand, and was more and more pleased as my work proceeded. What I most enjoyed was syllabifying the music to French, as I had done for Russian in *Les Noces*, and for Latin in *Oedipus Rex*.

I worked at the music of *Perséphone* from May, 1933, till I finished it at the end of the year. In November I gave several concerts in Spain. At Barcelona, at a festival which I conducted, I had the joy of presenting my son Sviatoslav to the public for the first time. He played my *Capriccio*. He made his Paris debut a year later with the symphony orchestra, when he played the *Capriccio* and my *Concerto pour Piano* under my direction.

In March, 1934, having finished the orchestral score, I was able to undertake a journey to Copenhagen to play my *Capriccio* for the radio, and I then made a concert tour with Dushkin in Lithuania and Latvia. On my return to Paris,

I took part in one of Siohan's concerts. He had recently been put in charge of the chorus at the Opera. He had already had the chorus make a careful study of the several parts of *Perséphone*, so that when I started rehearsals I found them very well prepared. As for the orchestra, it was, as usual, at the top of its form. But, again as usual, I had no end of trouble over the fatal custom of deputizing. There may be some justification for it when the current opera repertory is in question, but it is absurd and harmful when the work is not in the ordinary program, is wholly unknown to the musicians, and is to be given only a few times. *Perséphone* was given only three times at the Paris Opera – on April 30 and May 4 and 9, 1934. My participation was limited to conducting the music. The scenic effects were created without consulting me. I should like here to express my appreciation of the efforts made by Kurt Jooss, as master choreographer, and my regret that the poet was absent both from rehearsals and the actual performances. But the incident is all too recent for me to discuss it with the necessary detachment.

On the other hand, I was completely satisfied when I conducted *Perséphone* at a B.B.C. concert in London at the end of 1934. Mme Ida Rubinstein lent her valuable services, and so did René Maison, the excellent tenor who, with his musical flair, had so admirably rendered the songs of Eumolpus at the Paris performances.

Now that I have spoken about my last big composition, I have brought my chronicle almost up to date, and it is time to end it. Have I attained the objective I set before myself as described in my foreword? Have I given the reader a true picture of myself? Have I dispelled all the misconceptions which have accumulated about my work and my personality? I hope so.

The reader will have discovered that my book is not a

diary. He will not have found any lyrical outpourings or intimate confessions. I have deliberately avoided all that sort of thing. Where I have spoken of my tastes, my likes and dislikes, it has been only so far as was necessary to indicate what are my ideas, my convictions, and my point of view, and to describe my attitude towards other mentalities. In short, I have striven to set forth without any ambiguity what I hold to be the truth.

It would be vain, also, to seek in these pages for any aesthetic doctrine, a philosophy of art, or even a romantic description of the pangs experienced by the musician in giving birth to his creations, or of his rapture when the muse brings him inspiration. For me, as a creative musician, composition is a daily function that I feel compelled to discharge. I compose because I am made for that and cannot do otherwise. Just as any organ atrophies unless kept in a state of constant activity, so the faculty of composition becomes enfeebled and dulled unless kept up by effort and practice. The uninitiated imagine that one must await inspiration in order to create. That is a mistake. I am far from saying that there is no such thing as inspiration; quite the opposite. It is found as a driving force in every kind of human activity, and is in no wise peculiar to artists. But that force is only brought into action by an effort, and that effort is work. Just as appetite comes by eating, so work brings inspiration, if inspiration is not discernible at the beginning. But it is not simply inspiration that counts; it is the result of inspiration – that is, the composition.

At the beginning of my career as a composer I was a good deal spoiled by the public. Even such things as were at first received with hostility were soon afterwards acclaimed. But I have a very distinct feeling that in the course of the last fifteen years my written work has estranged me from the great mass of my listeners. They expected something different from me. Liking the music of *L'Oiseau de Feu*, *Petroushka*, *Le Sacre*, and *Les Noces*, and being accustomed to the language of those works, they are astonished to hear me speaking in another idiom. They cannot and will not follow me in the progress of my musical thought. What moves and delights me leaves them indifferent, and what still continues to interest them holds no further attraction for me. For that matter, I believe that there was seldom any real communion of spirit between us. If it happened – and it still happens – that we liked the same things, I very much doubt whether it was for the same reasons. Yet art postulates communion, and the artist has an imperative need to make others share the joy which he experiences himself. But, in spite of that need, he prefers direct and frank opposition to apparent agreement which is based on misunderstanding.

Unfortunately, perfect communion is rare, and the more the personality of the author is revealed the rarer that communion becomes. The more he eliminates all that is extraneous, all that is not his own, or "in him," the greater is his risk of conflicting with the expectations of the bulk of the public, who always receive a shock when confronted by something to which they are not accustomed.

The author's need for communion is all-embracing, but unfortunately that is only an unattainable ideal, so that he is compelled to content himself with something less. In my own case, I find that while the general public no longer gives me the enthusiastic reception of earlier days, that does not in any way prevent a large number of listeners, mainly of the young generation, from acclaiming my work with all the old ardor. I wonder whether, after all, it is simply a matter of the generation?

It is very doubtful whether Rimsky-Korsakov would

ever have accepted *Le Sacre*, or even *Petroushka*. Is it any wonder, then, that the hypercritics of today should be dumfounded by a language in which all the characteristics of their aesthetic seem to be violated? What, however, is less justifiable is that they nearly always blame the author for what is in fact due to their own lack of comprehension, a lack made all the more conspicuous because in their inability to state their grievance clearly they cautiously try to conceal their incompetence in the looseness and vagueness of their phraseology.

Their attitude certainly cannot make me deviate from my path. I shall assuredly not sacrifice my predilections and my aspirations to the demands of those who, in their blindness, do not realize that they are simply asking me to go backwards. It should be obvious that what they wish for has become obsolete for me, and that I could not follow them without doing violence to myself. But, on the other hand, it would be a great mistake to regard me as an adherent of *Zukunftsmusik* – the music of the future. Nothing could be more ridiculous. I live neither in the past nor in the future. I am in the present. I cannot know what tomorrow will bring forth. I can know only what the truth is for me today. That is what I am called upon to serve, and I serve it in all lucidity.